ALL ABOUT THE ROYAL FAMILY

BY PHOEBE HICHENS

AVON
PUBLISHERS OF BARD, CAMELOT, DISCUS AND FLARE BOOKS

Cover photograph of Prince Charles, Princess Diana and Prince William courtesy of Colour Library International (USA) Limited.

The following cover photographs also appear in the text:
Courtesy of Anwar Hussein, London, England: Queen riding in procession (p. 71), Prince Charles (p. 115).
Courtesy of Fox Photos, London, England: Coronation (p. 74), Princess Anne's Wedding (p. 75).
Camera Press, London, England: Prince Charles (p. 95), Anne and Philip (p. 99), Philip (p. 110), Queen (p. 111), Lady Diana (p. 115)

Art Director—Julian Holland
Design and Research—Rosemary Oxley
Picture Researcher—Sandra Assersohn
Editor—Caroline Adams
Illustrated by Leslie Marshall M.S.I.A.D.

Composition by Filmtype Services Limited, Scarborough, England

AVON BOOKS
A division of
The Hearst Corporation
1790 Broadway
New York, New York 10019

Library of Congress Cataloging in Publication Data

Hichens, Phoebe.
  All about the royal family.

  Bibliography
  Includes index.
  Summary: A compilation of miscellany about Great Britain's royal family over the centuries and about important places and buildings in the monarchy's history.
  1. Elizabeth II, Queen of Great Britain, 1926-
2. Great Britain—Kings and rulers—Biography.
3. Great Britain—Princes and princesses—Biography.
4. Great Britain—History. [1. Great Britain—Kings and rulers—Miscellanea. 2. Kings, queens, rulers, etc.—Miscellanea] I. Title.
DA590.H5   1983   941.085'092'4 [B]   83-12218
ISBN 0-380-64816-4

First Avon Printing, October, 1983

AVON TRADEMARK REG. U.S. PAT. OFF. AND IN OTHER COUNTRIES, MARCA REGISTRADA, HECHO EN U.S.A.

Printed in the U.S.A.

COM   10 9 8 7 6 5 4 3 2 1

Acknowledgments

The author would like to give her special thanks first and foremost to Mrs Anne Wall, of the Buckingham Palace Press Office who shared her encyclopaedic knowledge of the Royal Family and gave unstinting help on numerous occasions.

Thanks also to Sue Holland for making the cake on pages 86-7; the children of the following schools for their poetry and drawings (especially Peter and Polly Oxley): Ashford Church of England School, Ashford, Kent; Bousfield School, London; schools attached to the American airbase, Upper Heyford; the Steeple Aston Primary School; and King's College, Wimbledon; the photographers Patrick Kingston and Keith Ewart for their interest and assistance; and thanks to the London Library for their kindness and help.

The pictures on pages 8, 17, 40, 41, 42, 43, 44 left, 45, 46-7 top, bottom left and centre, 49 right, 50 left are reproduced by gracious permission of Her Majesty The Queen.

The publishers are also grateful to the following for permission to reproduce the pictures:
Aerofilms Ltd pages 16 bottom, 24, 28, cover bottom right; Hardy Amies Ltd page 107; Associated Newspapers Ltd page 68; BBC copyright pages 50 right, 72 left, 92, 95 top, 97 bottom right; BBC Hulton Picture Library pages 29, 33 bottom, 49 centre, 65, 89, 90 right, 91 left and right, 96 top and bottom left, 98 left, 99 top left and bottom right, 109 left; Barnaby's Picture Library pages 25, 26
Cecil Beaton page 47 centre
Trustees of the late Earl of Berkeley and Courtauld Institute of Art page 7 top
British Museum (Natural History) and Dr J. D. Bradley pages 46 left, 47 right
British Tourist Authority page 33 top
Trustees of the Broadlands Archives Trust page 96 bottom right
The Duke of Buccleuch and Queensberry, K.T. page 7 bottom

Camera Press pages 49 left, 62, 67, 80 bottom, 93 top, 115, (Annigoni) 11, (Baron) 98 right, (Cecil Beaton) 85 left, (Colin Davey) 106 left, (Andrew Davidson) 64 left, (Srdja Djukanovic) 104 left, (Peter Grugeon) 110 and 111, (Patrick Lichfield) 79 bottom, 97 top right, 99 top centre, 102, 114 bottom left, (Norman Parkinson) 115 top and bottom left, 116 and 117, (Bill Potter) 93 bottom left, (R. Slade) 95 bottom, (Studio Lisa) 10, 94, 100, (John Vaughan) 47 left
Central Press Photos pages 73 right, 77, 97 top centre, 101, 105 right, 120-1
Mary Evans Picture Library pages 18, 90 left
Fox Photos pages 44 right, 55, 64 centre, 66 top, 69 top left, right and bottom, 70, 74, 74-5, 75 left, 76-7, 93 bottom right, 95 left, 97 top left, 103, 108, 125, cover bottom left
Stanley Gibbons International Ltd page 9 left
Eric Hosking page 97 bottom left
Anwar Hussein pages 2, 3, 66 bottom, 66-7, 71, 78, 78-9, 79 top, 99 bottom left and top right, 106 centre and right, 114 top and bottom right, 123, cover top centre
Imperial War Museum page 91 centre
ITC Entertainment page 49 right
A. F. Kersting pages 21, 32
Keystone Press Agency pages 75 right, 76, 105 left
Patrick Kingston page 79 right
Serge Lemoine pages 73 left, 81
Pitkin Pictorials page 39
Popperfoto pages 64 right, 72 right, 80 top and bottom, 97 bottom centre
Press Association pages 34-5
Andrew Robb and Robert Harding Associates page 109 right
Spink & Son page 9 right
Controller of Her Majesty's Stationery Office pages 82, 83, cover bottom centre
John Topham Picture Library pages 18-19, 85 right
The Zoological Society of London page 104 right

Although every care has been taken to acknowledge the correct sources for the photographs reproduced in this book, the publishers wish to apologize to anyone whose copyright they may have unknowingly infringed.

Contents

Introduction

It would take many books to cover the whole story of the British Monarchy, past and present. But, thanks to a special team of helpers, it has been possible to compile a new and special guide to the subject. Quite simply, it is a guide dealing with the facts that are *most interesting* to young people.

Children of all ages and of many different nationalities made up our team. They filled in questionnaires, wrote essays, composed poems, drew pictures. (Some of these are featured in the book.) And all this helped us to choose favourite subjects and answer favourite questions.

It was also important to make the guide as accurate as possible. Historical facts have been checked by a well-known historian. And we asked the Press Office at Buckingham Palace to co-operate in our research and help to check much of the present day information.

We believe the research has produced a guide to the Royal Family that is both reliable and fresh, factual and lively. To all the helpers who joined us in this tremendously enjoyable project – a very warm thank you.

May 12th 1546

Pardon my rude style in writing to you, most illustrious Queen and beloved mother, and receive my hearty thanks for your loving kindness to me and my sister. Yet, dearest Mother, the only true consolation is from Heaven and the only real love is the love of God. Preserve, therefore, I pray you my dear sister Mary from all the wiles and enchantments of the evil one, and beseech her to attend no longer to foreign dances and merriments which do not become a Christian princess.

Edward VI, aged 9. (To Catherine Parr.)

Sweet sweet Father,

I learn to decline substantives and adjectives. Give me your blessing.

Charles I, aged 8. (To James I.)

My Lord, I would not have you take too much physick for it doth always make me worse and I think it will do the like to you.

Charles II, aged 9. (To Lord Newcastle.)

April 17th 1876

My dear Grandmamma,

I hope you are enjoying yourself very much in Germany as we are all doing here . . . Please thank Aunt Beatrice very much for the nice chocolate egg she sent me yesterday. Mama gave us some very pretty Easter eggs with lots of nice little things inside them, and ones which we had to find to the sound of music played loud when we were near and soft when we were far off. We went this morning to the farm to see some Brahmin cows which dear Papa sent home from India and we fed them with biscuits.

George V, aged 11. (To Victoria.)

BUCKINGHAM PALACE

14th December, 1937

Darling Grannie,

Thank you very much for those lovely Coronation mugs.

When we lifted them out of the box, they both began playing "God Save the King" at different parts!

Aunt Mary enrolled us last night and everything went off very well and we were all terribly nervous while we waited but when Aunt Mary came in we could see she was very nervous also. Then we felt quite at home.

We all want to thank you very much for all those wonderful Monday afternoons we have had this term.

With love from your very loving grandaughters,
Lilibet & Margaret

York Cottage.
December 15th, 1903.

Dear Papa and Mama,

Thank you very much indeed for the letters, telegram and presents, which I like very much. I had a lovely day. We played about till 11.30, when we went to Sandringham and saw my table. We played golf in the afternoon and at five o'clock we went to tea with Grannie in the big dining room. Then we all moved into the hall, where we found a man ready with a big magic lantern, which had three lenses. Then Mr. Bertram, the Conjurer, did a number of tricks, which Harry liked very much.

With very best love,
I remain
ever your affectionate son
Bertie

Brussells. Sept. 20th 1679

I went to see a ball at the court incognito which I liked very well. It was in very good order and some danced well enough. Indeed there was a Prince Vaudemont that danced extremely well, as well if not better than either Sir E. Villiers or the Duke of Monmouth which I think very extraordinary . . . As for the town, it is a great and fine town. Methinks though the streets are not so clean as they are in Holland, yet they are not as dirty as ours . . . They only have odd kinds of smells.

Anne I, aged 15. (To Lady Apsley.)

Sovereign Queens

I think it was Boadicea who decided women ought to be queens, but the men said no and she got cross and poisoned her daughters.

Henry. 10. English

Some men, it is true, have not liked the idea of a woman ruler. When James V of Scotland died, leaving only a daughter ". . . all men lamented that the realm was left without a male to succeed." (John Knox)

Yet women did become Monarchs or Sovereigns. They inherited the Crown and ruled the country in their own right. This usually happened, when there were no surviving brothers, or children of their brothers. But other British titles, like duke, earl or baronet, hardly ever pass to women; so it is surprising that they should have had a right to the title of Sovereign, which is the highest title of all. It is even more surprising that they should have had this right for so long.

Boudicca was Queen of a British tribe who fought the Romans. (There is a legend that when she knew she would lose, she poisoned herself and her daughters.) That was nearly 2,000 years ago. It was not until 1135 AD that a woman, Matilda, claimed the Crown of all England.

Matilda. (*Born 1102, died 1167. Daughter of Henry I.*)

When King Henry's son and heir, Prince William, was drowned in the *White Ship*, the only legitimate child left to Henry was a daughter. He forced his barons to accept her as heir to the throne. But after his death, many broke their oath and supported her cousin, Stephen, instead.

There were men who fought hard for Matilda's rights. But in the end Stephen was crowned and Matilda was forced to flee from a besieged Oxford Castle. One snowy day, she and four attendants, wrapped in white sheets, slipped like ghosts through the guards, crossed the frozen river on foot and escaped!

Queen Matilda escaping from Oxford Castle with her attendants.

Lady Jane Grey. (*Born 1537. Executed 1554. Granddaughter of Henry VII.*)

Edward VI named Jane his heir. His sister Mary had a better claim to the throne but some nobles preferred Jane because she was a Protestant. Jane's father, the Duke of Suffolk, and her father-in-law, the Duke of Northumberland, led those who supported her.

When Edward died, fifteen-year-old Jane and her young husband, Guildford, were taken to the Tower in the Royal Barge. They were greeted with a great fanfare of trumpets, and heralds proclaimed Jane queen. She was crowned. But all over England people were rising in support of Mary, who was Henry VIII's eldest daughter, and the rightful queen.

After nine days, Jane's supporters knew they had lost. Her father came to the Council Chamber where she was sitting on the throne. He told her to come down: "That is no place for you." Jane said, "Can I go home?"

A few months later, the girl, who was one of the most brilliant scholars of her time, was taken to the scaffold. She was only sixteen; but as a royal princess she was expected to face execution with dignity. She was also expected to make a speech. The small, sandy haired girl, on her way to her death, did what was expected of her.

She made a speech beginning, "Good people, I am come here to die," and she asked the crowd to witness that she died a true Christian. She recited a psalm and forgave her executioner. The only moment of uncertainty came when she blindfolded herself and could not find her way to the block. "Where is it? What am I to do?" she said. An onlooker helped her to find her way, she laid down her head on the block and the axe fell.

Mary I. (*Born 1516. Reigned 1553 to 1558. Daughter of Henry VIII and his first wife, Katherine of Aragon.*)

Mary was a clever and loving daughter. Henry called her: "his chiefest Jewel". Then Henry divorced her mother and she was neglected by her father and bullied by her step-mother, Anne Boleyn. Mary became bitter and unhappy.

As queen, she made an unpopular marriage to Philip of Spain. She loved her husband but he thought her dull and middle-aged. She decided that her unhappy marriage was a punishment from God because she had not done enough for the Catholic religion. So she began to persecute Protestants and many were burned as heretics. Her subjects nick-named her "Bloody Mary".

A miniature of Mary I. She had an unsuccessful and unhappy reign and was nicknamed "Bloody Mary" by her subjects.

Elizabeth I playing the lute. The Tudors were a very musical family and learned to play instruments at a young age.

Elizabeth I. (*Born 1533. Reigned 1558 to 1603. Daughter of Henry VIII and his second wife, Anne Boleyn.*)

Elizabeth was the first great Sovereign Queen of England. She was also the last British queen to rule with great power. She could make laws and order the execution or torture of anyone she considered dangerous. Although she might listen to the advice of her Parliament, she did not have to take their advice. In fact, during the 45 years of her reign, Parliament only sat for 22 months. However, her commonsense policies and political skills made her popular with her people throughout her long reign.

Elizabeth's early life was even more difficult and dangerous than Mary's had been. Elizabeth's mother was beheaded and Elizabeth herself had to pass through Traitor's Gate knowing that the axe might fall on her own neck. But the young princess learned a great deal; to keep a cool head, to talk her way out of trouble and to charm her enemies.

Elizabeth had her faults. She was vain and loved flattery. She lied when it suited her, and encouraged many suitors. In her old age she must have seemed an absurd figure: overdressed, over-jewelled and heavily made up. But her virtues outshone her faults. She understood, perhaps better than any Monarch before her, that Sovereigns must deserve the great power they possess.

Her great strength was built on the goodwill of her people. She realized that violence, bloodshed and persecution would not pay and that the people would follow the Sovereign they loved, not the tyrant they feared.

Elizabeth I out hawking. Like her father, Henry VIII, Elizabeth was a keen rider and sportswoman.

7

Sir Walter Raleigh gained favour with Elizabeth I when he spread his cloak over a puddle at her feet.

Elizabeth had seen England torn apart by religious war between Catholics and Protestants. She made it clear that the days of persecution were largely over and people could worship without Royal interference. As a result the whole country united under her rule.

Elizabeth had one great rival, Mary Queen of Scots, whom she eventually had executed, as Mary claimed Elizabeth's own throne. The Scottish Queen was a Catholic and there were people of her own faith in England who were eager to support her. In spite of Mary's plotting, Elizabeth hesitated for years before having Mary executed.

Elizabeth established herself as a strong ruler in a ruthless age. She declared: "I know I have the body of a weak and feeble woman, but I have the heart and stomach of a King."

Mary II. (*Born 1662. Reigned jointly with her husband, William of Orange, from 1688 to 1694.*)

Royal power was never the same after the execution of Charles I. More and more it was Parliament which ruled; and when James II opposed his ministers he was quickly thrown out. His daughters, Mary and Anne, did not make the same mistake.

Mary relied greatly on her shrewd and politically experienced husband. She had none of Elizabeth's political genius, but she did possess a happy family life.

When Mary was dying of smallpox William stayed close to her, sleeping on a camp-bed in her bedroom. Later, William told Bishop Burnet, "She had no faults, none. You knew her well but you could not know, nobody but myself could know her goodness."

Anne. (*Born 1665. Reigned 1702 to 1714. Second daughter of James II.*)

Anne's husband, George of Denmark, had no interest in politics and it is to Good Queen Anne's credit that she kept a reasonable relationship between herself and the changing Parliament. She was not clever but, like her sister, she had commonsense.

Anne was not a glamorous queen. Her face grew spotty. Her legs swelled with gout and she became so fat that her coffin had to be almost as wide as it was long!

Anne was dull and conventional but she was sensible about the government and welfare of the country. She was kind and hardworking and people felt she did her best. Also she represented something that was to become important to the monarchy: a good family life.

Victoria. (*Born 1819. Reigned 1837 to 1901. Daughter of the Duke of Kent and niece of George IV and William IV.*)

It must have been like a fairytale for Victoria. One moment the eighteen-year-old girl was strictly controlled by her mother and governess and not even allowed her own bedroom. Then suddenly, she was Queen. She could move into her own palace, order upholstery for her own throne and interview the Prime Minister. Not since the return of Charles II had a new Monarch been greeted with such delight. The Hanoverians were not very popular and the crowds went wild when they saw the young Victoria.

A portrait of Queen Victoria as a young girl. Many people considered her to be very attractive.

Victoria was strong-willed, however, and very fond of getting her own way. She wanted to be a good queen, but she did not altogether understand how a good queen, reigning in the nineteenth century, ought to behave. Since the death of Anne, there had been more changes for the Monarchy. Victoria was now a constitutional Monarch, and this meant, quite simply, that she had no right to govern the country or interfere in politics.

Anne had presided over meetings of the Cabinet and she could argue, openly, in favour of a particular law. But the Queen's place in the Cabinet had now been taken by the Prime Minister; and Victoria was left with only three clear rights. She had the right to be consulted, the right to encourage and the right to warn. She must be told about everything that went on; she could give advice behind the scenes; but she had no real power.

Victoria did not always keep these rules. She made no secret of her likes and dislikes. She openly preferred Melbourne and Disraeli to Peel and Gladstone when they were Prime Ministers. (She once wrote such a rude letter to Gladstone that he nearly resigned.)

She tried to change new laws and sometimes even succeeded. She refused to include a man in the Cabinet because he was a gambler and had lived with his wife before they were married.

Luckily her husband, Albert, prevented a serious crisis. He understood the rules for a constitutional monarch, and, in time, he persuaded Victoria to behave more sensibly.

At first the young queen had been so self-confident that even her husband had been kept in his place. But she came to rely on him more and more and eventually people even called her "Queen Albertine".

After Albert's death, Victoria retreated to Balmoral to mourn and for years refused to take part in public life. Again, this was against the rules. The Monarch remained, above all, the representative of the country. She had to be seen to be respected and had Victoria died in retirement she would not be remembered as a great queen. But Victoria emerged, and established a bond with her people. "The British have always liked Kings and Queens, particularly the old ones," wrote Ian, a 12-year-old Scot.

Queen Victoria reading letters in the grounds of Osborne House. With her is John Brown, who had been Albert's servant. She relied on him for help and advice in many matters. One wild rumour had it that they had been secretly married!

The older Victoria became, the more she represented something firm and familiar in a changing world. Everyone knew that she believed in God, marriage and family life as firmly at eighty as she had done at eighteen.

Early English Kings, like Edward III, Henry II and Henry V, had certainly become famous in Europe. The fame of Elizabeth I — thanks to her great sailors and explorers — had spread as far as the Americas. (George III had become thoroughly infamous in America!) But Victoria was the first British Queen whose name spread to all four corners of the globe. And it was more than a name. Victoria became a symbol of strength and unity to millions of people — many of whom lived thousands of miles away.

This was the reign when the sun never set on the British Empire. And in the faraway countries of India, Australia, Canada and Africa, it was not the great British statesmen like Disraeli or Gladstone or Palmerston who appeared as the symbol of British rule and justice. They were always changing. The real representative of the Mother Country was a dumpy little woman dressed in widow's black. It was the wonderfully familiar, unchanging figure of Queen Victoria. Others might come and go; but this was the figure that seemed to go on for ever and ever.

Penny Black stamps, from Victoria's reign, are now valuable items in stamp collections.

A Victorian coin. These coins were still in circulation until decimalization in 1971.

Elizabeth II. *(Born 1926. Crowned 1953. Daughter of George VI.)*

Elizabeth I was outstanding as a ruling Queen. She seemed to be exactly what the country needed at that particular time. Most people feel that Elizabeth II is an outstanding constitutional Queen. She is what is wanted and needed in this particular age.

Yet the two women could hardly be less alike. Elizabeth I was a brilliant scholar, a wheeler and dealer, sometimes a liar and always a flirt. Elizabeth II is intelligent but not scholarly. She is respected by Heads of State for her total honesty and sincerity. She has no desire for dozens of suitors: she fell in love with Prince Philip in her early teens and never looked at another man. Nor does she share Elizabeth I's love of flattery.

Elizabeth I adored clothes and finery. Elizabeth II knows it is part of her job to be well-dressed and, for that reason, gives care and thought to her wardrobe. But, left to herself, she is probably happiest in tweeds and knitwear. "I can't wear all that," she protested when she saw the ball gown, tiara and jewellery laid out for her first official banquet as Monarch.

But the Elizabeths do have two important things in common. They are both courageous. Elizabeth I was told it was too dangerous for her to go to the coast and address her men before the Spanish Armada. She paid no attention and went. Elizabeth II was told it was too dangerous for her to visit Northern Ireland in her Jubilee Year, 1977. She insisted on going.

Even more important, the second Elizabeth understands, just as well as the first, that she must rely on the goodwill of the people. Elizabeth I called this goodwill and loyalty her "chiefest strength"; Elizabeth II would agree.

Elizabeth is a much better constitutional Monarch than Victoria and this earns her goodwill. No doubt she does like some ministers more than others. Perhaps she does argue about political matters behind the scenes. But her discretion is near perfect. She is never seen to interfere in the rights of Parliament or to favour any one political party.

"Her Majesty ... was most talkative and amusing," wrote Marie Mallett, Maid of Honour to Victoria. "Indeed Mary Hughes and I had much ado to keep from immoderate laughter." The same is true of Elizabeth II. She can look very severe but people meeting her for the first time are surprised to find she has a marvellous sense of humour.

In some ways, Elizabeth resembles her great-great-grandmother, Victoria. They share the same honesty, the same devotion to husband and family, and a strong religious belief. There is the same royal dignity in public, but the ability to be relaxed, affectionate and often funny in private although an outsider might never see this more informal side.

The Princesses Elizabeth and Margaret playing with the family corgis in the grounds of the Royal Lodge, Windsor. Corgis have been a favourite breed with the Royal Family since the first royal corgi was bought by George VI – then Duke of York – in 1933. The Queen now owns a number of corgis.

Elizabeth knows no Sovereign can take his or her throne for granted. She has not, like Anne and Mary, seen her father deposed and her grandfather beheaded. But she has seen her uncle, Edward VIII, forced to choose between the Crown and the woman he wanted to marry. She has seen royal families all over Europe thrown out of their countries. (Her own husband and his family were among them.)

But after the triumph of her Jubilee Year, Elizabeth must feel that she has earned the goodwill of her people. They believe that her whole heart is in her work.

Jubilees are quite a recent royal occasion. Few of the early Monarchs lived long enough to celebrate twenty-five, let alone fifty or sixty years of reign. George III was the first to celebrate a Golden Jubilee; but as he was blind and ill, it was not a happy occasion and he did not even appear.

Victoria refused to celebrate her Silver Jubilee because she was still in mourning for Albert, who had died the year before.

But her Golden and Diamond Jubilees were tremendous occasions. Both times, the weather was perfect. (People began to call fine weather "the Queen's weather".) A great wave of rejoicing with parties and pageants and bonfires swept the country. Forty Royal Princes rode in the procession of the Golden Jubilee.

The Queen Empress entertained royalty and statesmen from numerous countries. "Go it, old girl!" shouted a man in the crowds at her Diamond Jubilee. It was the voice of true affection.

Although the glory of the Empire was fading, and the danger of the Second World War growing, the same affection burst out at the Jubilee of George V.

The King — a gruff, rather shy man — was overcome by the delight of the great crowds who greeted him wherever he went with cheers and waving flags. After one such reception in the East End he said, "I had no idea they felt like that about me. I am beginning to think they must like me for myself." The streets were decorated too, and the whole country celebrated.

Annigoni's portrait of the Queen was painted in 1954. It was commissioned by the Worshipful Company of Fishmongers.

But in some ways, the Jubilee of Elizabeth II was the greatest triumph of all. It was at a time when Britain's power and prestige were only a shadow of the great Victorian days and many other monarchies had collapsed.

The whole idea of royalty might have seemed out of date and out of place in a modern world. Yet love for the Queen broke out stronger than ever. Every country in the Commonwealth greeted her visits with joy. And the whole of Britain suddenly had the atmosphere of one huge celebration. Banners appeared everywhere. "Betty rules — okay?" "Great going, Liz!" On the day itself, 7,000 messages poured into Buckingham Palace. The police said they hoped they wouldn't come across any anti-monarchists. "We would have to arrest them — for their own protection!"

Queen Elizabeth is no actress. She can only look truly happy when she feels truly happy. And most people would agree with Jim, aged 10, who wrote: "I know she had a smashing time at her Jubilee because she kept smiling as if she couldn't help smiling." It was obvious that the Queen, dressed in brilliant pink, was radiantly happy. And as she passed through the cheering crowds, perhaps she had the same thought as her grandfather, "I had no idea they felt like that about me."

Even as a child, Elizabeth had been taught she must try hard, harder than other little girls, because she represented something big and important. But it's impossible to feel she would ever have chosen another life.

"When I was twenty-one," she said, "I pledged my life to the service of our people and I asked God's help to make good that vow . . . I do not regret nor retract one word of it."

It was the same promise made at her Coronation. A bishop was to say: "The most wonderful thing I ever saw in my life was the moment when she lifted the sword and laid it on the altar — she was putting her whole heart and soul to the service of the people."

Palaces of the Past

Kings and Queens thought it was royal to have an awful lot of palaces.

Mark, 9. English

Elizabeth I had fourteen palaces and castles in regular use. Her ancestor, Edward I, had many more. The further back in history you go, the more residences the Monarch owned. William the Conqueror would be astonished to learn that our present Queen only has three palaces at her disposal. (This does not, of course, include the property which she owns herself.)

In the old days, palaces were needed for many different reasons. Monarchs had to travel around their kingdoms to see that their laws were obeyed and that their position as Sovereign was secure. They also went in search of food for themselves and for their courts.

Palaces were used as forts and prisons as well as royal residences. Sometimes they began as hideaways: places where the Monarch hoped to get away from the pressure of court life. In the end, the court would always follow, and the holiday home, as it expanded, would become an official palace.

There are more royal homes scattered around Britain than could ever be counted, though some have disappeared beneath the earth forever. We will begin by describing the more famous of these vanished palaces.

CAMELOT

Great palaces have vanished under the earth; but it is usually known where they stood. We even have some idea of the way they looked. But nobody knows the site of King Arthur's palace. Some historians have placed it at Winchester, others at South Cadbury in Somerset, others in London. But there is no definite proof.

Nor do we know for certain what the palace of Camelot looked like. Legends talk of a great flat field near to the castle where the knights practised their fighting skills and where tournaments were held. They also mention a forest, a river and, of course, the Round Table. But the Round Table is the only distinctive feature. Fields and forests and rivers can be found close to many palaces.

The story of Arthur, the half-magical king and hero, is a marvellous one, but it may well be only a legend. We do not know for certain that he existed. The same must be said of Camelot, as the palace has vanished without trace.

An artist's impression of Camelot. No-one knows what the palace looked like.

FISHBOURNE

Fishbourne is believed to be the first great palace ever built in Britain. It was so enormous that it would have made Buckingham Palace look small by comparison.

It was built by the Romans around 75 AD, near the present town of Chichester; and it was probably given to a local king, called Cogidubnus. He had sided with the Roman invaders and helped them to conquer the west of England. This was his reward.

The building covered six acres and surrounded a beautiful garden. The walls were inlaid with costly Greek and Turkish marble and there were shining mosaic floors. The most famous mosaic is a picture of Cupid riding a dolphin, surrounded by sea monsters. The Romans liked to be comfortable, and they installed a huge bath suite and central heating system — quite different to the simple palaces of British kings.

Fishbourne was burnt to the ground around 270 AD and the site was not discovered until 1960.

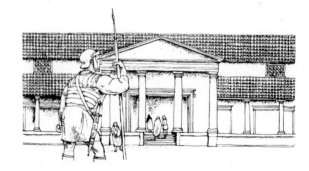

The entrance to the audience chamber at Fishbourne. Fishbourne was the first great palace ever to be built in Britain. It was bigger than Buckingham Palace, the Queen's residence today.

The palace of Winchester. It was here that Alfred composed the Anglo-Saxon Chronicle, the first history of Britain.

WINCHESTER

There were two palaces at Winchester. The first was built by the Saxon king, Alfred, the second by the Norman, William I. They were not nearly as grand as Fishbourne. Alfred's palace, built in the ninth century, was said to be very damp and unhealthy. The first Norman kings thought of castles and palaces as forts to be defended against enemies rather than comfortable places for themselves and their families to live.

But William's palace did contain a famous picture, commissioned by Henry II. The picture showed four young eagles attacking the parent eagle. "The four eaglets," said Henry, "are my four sons who cease not to persecute me, even unto death." And so they did!

It Happened Here

Alfred started the Anglo Saxon Chronicle at Winchester. It was the first history book written for the English people in their own language. It covered the years 55 BC to 1154 AD. The chronicle was probably chained up in Winchester Cathedral so that anyone could read it if they wanted to.

Under William I, the records, the mint, the royal treasures and Domesday Book were stored in the Norman palace traditionally under the King's bed!

WOODSTOCK

This palace was built as a hunting lodge for Henry I. He surrounded it with a great stone wall, seven miles long. The land inside was turned into a deer park and zoo. Henry often asked foreign kings for lions, leopards, camels and other strange beasts.

The hunting lodge grew into a palace; and was eventually given by Queen Anne to the Duke of Marlborough as a reward for his great victory at the Battle of Blenheim. But the Duke's architect decided the old buildings were "altogether ruinous" and they were abandoned.

It Happened Here

Henry II was said to have a love affair with a famous beauty, "the fair Rosamund", at Woodstock. Legend says that his jealous Queen, Eleanor, murdered her.

The young Elizabeth was imprisoned here by Mary I.

The palace of Woodstock. It was said to contain a secret maze.

The banqueting hall of Whitehall. This is all that is left of what was once the largest palace in Europe.

WHITEHALL

This was once the largest palace in Europe, covering twenty-three acres. (Versailles only covered seven acres, the Vatican Palace in Rome, less than fourteen acres.)

Whitehall began as the London residence of the Archbishops of York. When Wolsey became Archbishop under Henry VIII, he enlarged the building and furnished it luxuriously. The palace was so magnificent that Henry became jealous, took it for himself and made Whitehall a royal palace.

From then on, until the reign of William and Mary, Whitehall was the centre of court life. In appearance, it was more like a village than a single palace; with many different buildings, gardens, walks and sports centres. There were separate lodgings for courtiers, as well as the royal apartments. There were tennis courts, bowling alleys, a ball house (where a form of badminton was played), a cockpit for fighting animals and a tilt yard where the knights in armour could practise.

In 1698, a careless servant left some linen to dry beside a big charcoal fire and it caught light. The flames raced from building to building and raged uncontrollably for seventeen days. In the end, very little of the royal village of Whitehall was left standing.

It Happened Here
Shakespeare's plays were performed before Elizabeth I.

On a bitterly cold January day, Charles I was executed.

Elizabeth, wife of Oliver Cromwell, installed secret passages and trapdoors so that she could spy on her servants.

The ancient rite of "Touching for the King's Evil" was performed in the Banqueting House. For centuries, a touch of the royal hand was said to cure disease. Charles II is believed to have touched nearly 100,000 people.

Henry VIII arrived in disguise at a fabulous party at Whitehall, given by Wolsey. He and his companions were disguised as foreign ambassadors who happened to be in the country. It was a favourite joke of the King's to appear at parties in a disguise.

Whitehall was a great place for masques. Queen Anne, wife of James I, loved to dress up; and in one evening she appeared as a goddess, a nymph, a Turkish Sultana and an Indian Princess.

Charles II weighed himself after a strenuous game of tennis. He was pleased to find he had lost four and a half pounds.

When she became queen, Mary II arrived at Whitehall "laughing and jolly as to a wedding". Some people felt, out of respect to her newly deposed father, she should have behaved more soberly.

The fabulous palace of Nonsuch, said to be the place where Elizabeth I took her infrequent baths.

The outer gatehouse, Nonsuch Palace. Henry VIII built the palace. He had endless problems with the builders.

NONSUCH
Henry VIII was a great builder of palaces. This was the last and most extravagant of all. He pulled down an entire village in Surrey to get the necessary stone. Artists and craftsmen from all over Europe were employed. The building deserved the name "Nonsuch" which means "like nothing else on earth".

The palace was built around two courtyards. The outer courtyard was in plain Tudor style; the inner, an extravagance of gold and white. There was a vast marble fountain, the basin of which was held up by golden griffins, and surmounted by a galloping marble horse. There was a spectacular statue of Henry VIII, glittering on a burnished throne. The walls were covered with brilliant white plaster, moulded into life-size scenes of Mount Olympus and the labours of Hercules. Round the upper buildings were thirty-one figures of Roman emperors and the gardens were full of marble animals. There was a great maze, an orchard, a dark wood and a Grove of Diana, with another dramatic fountain.

Nonsuch was the palace to which Henry planned to retire; but it was not finished until after his death. Elizabeth I was the only Monarch who liked the palace. Charles II gave it away to his mistress, Barbara Villiers; and she passed it on to property developers. The palace was demolished and now lies beneath the suburbs of Surrey.

It Happened Here
Elizabeth I was said to take her (very infrequent) baths in the Grove of Diana.

Bishop Aylmer preached a tactless sermon in front of Queen Elizabeth I criticizing people who "decked the body too finely". Elizabeth, decked in her usual extravagant clothes and finery was none too pleased with him!

Elizabeth's young favourite, the Earl of Essex, rushed from Ireland after a disastrous war, to beg the Queen's forgiveness at Nonsuch. He burst into the Queen's bedroom and found her without her wig, make-up, court dress or jewellery. He was later beheaded.

14

A river-side view of Richmond Palace. The gardens were famous for the lions and dragons carved from the yew hedges.

RICHMOND

This was one of the more comfortable palaces. Richard II installed separate lavatories instead of communal ones. There were also fireplaces in the smaller rooms.

It was a Tudor palace, enclosed by a mighty brick wall with many towers. The gold vanes, on top of each tower, were said to sing sweetly in the wind. The gardens were spectacular. In particular they were famous for the fabulous lions and dragons which were carved out of the massive yew hedges.

It Happened Here

Edward III died at Richmond, deserted by everyone but a poor priest.

Anne of Bohemia, first wife of Richard II, died here. The King was said to be very distressed by her death.

Richmond was sold in order to pay the Roundhead troops during the Civil War. Thereafter, the buildings were allowed to crumble and decay.

No More a Palace

Some palaces have stopped being particularly royal.

Joan, 12, Australian

There are palaces which have completely disappeared. Others survive, but they are no longer the residence of the Monarch. They may have become a museum, a centre of government or a residence for other members of the Royal Family. But they cannot be called an official palace, like Buckingham Palace or Windsor Castle.

The most famous ex-palace is the Tower of London.

THE TOWER OF LONDON

The Tower's proper title is still "Her Majesty's Royal Palace and Fortress of the Tower of London". But even in the early days, the accent was on "fortress" rather than "palace". As a royal home it was grimly uncomfortable (even today, the Governor's house is no model of luxury). But it was also immensely strong and easy to defend. In fact, it was an ideal retreat for the Monarch in times of trouble.

The famous White Tower — still the heart of the citadel — dates from about 1080 and its walls, up to five metres thick, contained the royal apartments and the Chapel of St John. They also contained dungeons.

As later kings strengthened and extended the fortifications, the palace expanded into a small 'town' with not one but twenty towers. There were shops and taverns and churches and up to 1,000 residents.

The royal fortress contained the Royal Mint, the Courts of Justice, a factory for making bows and arrows, the National Observatory and a zoo. Early in the fourteenth century, it housed the Crown Jewels and this is one use which has continued to the present day.

After the Middle Ages Monarchs were less concerned about their security and the Tower was abandoned as a royal residence. Today, Her Majesty's Royal Palace and Fortress is one of the greatest tourist attractions in the world, with around two million visitors a year.

Officers of the Tower

The Constable of the Tower was in command of the army garrison. A high ranking officer is still appointed to this title and he has direct access to the Monarch.

The Governor of the Tower continues to live on the premises. His other title is Keeper of the Jewel House. He is responsible for the Crown Jewels.

The famous executioner's block and a raven from the Tower of London.

Yeomen Warders are full-time guards. Their gold and scarlet uniforms are almost as famous as the Tower itself. One of these warders is the Raven Master. He is responsible for feeding the ravens and clipping their wings. There is a legend that the White Tower will fall if the ravens ever leave.

An old plan of the Tower (left). An aerial view of the Tower (below). The White Tower dates from 1078.

It Happened Here

King John imprisoned Maud, daughter of Lord Fitzwalter, in the Tower because she would not accept his love. He finally had her poisoned.

Isabella, wife of Edward II, lived in the Tower. She fell in love with one of the prisoners, Roger Mortimer, and helped him to escape. Later they deposed her husband and murdered him.

The Duke of Clarence, brother of Edward IV, is said to have been drowned in a barrel of Malmsey wine.

The two little sons of Edward IV were murdered here. It is possible that Henry VII was responsible. Another suspect is Richard III, their uncle.

A special swordsman was imported from France to behead Anne Boleyn at a cost of £23.

Margaret, Countess of Salisbury, was thought to have had the least dignified execution. She was chased round the block by the executioner.

Few people ever escaped from the Tower, but the Earl of Nithsdale succeeded. The evening before his execution, his wife and three women came to say goodbye. One had put on two dresses, another two cloaks. The Earl, disguised in the spare dress and cloak, and pretending to weep so as to keep his face covered, slipped out with the others.

In the reign of Richard II, rioting peasants broke into the Tower. They shook the knights by their beards, and went on into the king's Privy Chamber. Here they enjoyed themselves "sitting, lying and sporting on the king's bed". What's more, they saucily invited the king's mother to "kiss with them".

The last prisoner in the Tower was Rudolph Hess, Adolf Hitler's deputy.

ST JAMES PALACE

This palace started life, nearly 1,000 years ago, as a leper colony. By the time of Henry VIII there were only four lepers left. (Each received a yearly allowance of £2 12s and a quarter-barrel of beer.) Later, the old hospital was rebuilt as a royal hunting lodge, and also as a hideaway for King Henry's new love, Anne Boleyn.

Like Woodstock, it had many secret rooms and passages. It was probably a favourite place for the royal children to play hide-and-seek. Two children of Charles I, Princess Henrietta and Prince James, did indeed play hide-and-seek very cleverly. They were imprisoned here during the Civil War but they managed to escape.

Later, in the reign of Charles II, it was the

Inspecting the Yeomen of the Guard in Friery Court, at St James Palace in London.

ideal place for the King and his courtiers to carry on secret love affairs.

After Whitehall burned down, St James became the principal London palace; but after the move to Buckingham Palace, which began during George III's reign, no Monarch ever lived at St James again.

St James can still be called "royal" because it is the home of the Queen Mother and other members of the Royal Family. It is still the place where heralds proclaim the accession of a new **king** or queen.

It Happened Here

Prince Henry, son of James I, died here. Every remedy was tried to save him: and Walter Raleigh — then a prisoner in the Tower — sent round his own medicine. It was to cure everything but poison. It was also said it smelt like whisky.

Charles I spent the night before his execution at St James. He is said to have slept soundly.

Mary, second wife of James II, hurried here to give birth to her baby. As it was known to be a good place for secret comings and goings, many people believed a baby was smuggled in — perhaps in a warming pan — and presented, fraudulently, as heir to the throne. He continued to be known as "the warming-pan baby". After James II was deposed his son was known as the "Old Pretender".

George IV met his intended bride, Princess Caroline, here. She was said to suffer from body odour; and after he embraced her, George turned to the ambassador and said, "Harris, I am not well. Pray get me a glass of brandy."

In 1936, Mrs Simpson watched from a window as the heralds proclaimed the accession of Edward VIII.

The North front of St James Palace, which was once a royal hunting lodge.

A view of the interior of St James Palace. Several kings used the Palace to carry on their secret love affairs.

WESTMINSTER

There is a legend that the first palace of Westminster was built by Canute. Certainly, a palace — costing a tenth of his wealth — was built here by Edward the Confessor.

The ancient palace has become the centre of modern government. Even in the early days, Monarchs used Westminster as their business headquarters; but Henry VIII was glad to move out and, from then on, Westminster was left in the hands of government officials.

Links between Westminster and the Crown remained. Great coronation feasts were held there as late as the reign of George IV. The Sovereign is still crowned at Westminster Abbey. But the present Houses of Parliament are nothing like the palace of long ago. They do, however, still stand on the ancient foundations and preserve certain ancient traditions.

It Happened Here

Henry II had his most famous quarrel with Thomas Becket here.

In 1264, Simon de Montfort summoned prelates, barons and commons to Westminster Hall. It was the beginning of a democratic Parliament.

Richard II installed some of the earliest hot-and-cold water taps for his bath.

The Guy Fawkes plot failed.

Cromwell said of Charles I, "We will cut off his head with the crown on it."

GREENWICH

The land around Greenwich was owned by the Crown before the Norman Conquest. But the first great palace there was built by the brother of Henry V, Humphrey Duke of Gloucester.

By the time of Charles II, the old buildings were nearly derelict. Work was started on a great new palace, to be called The King's House; but this was never to be a royal residence. William and Mary handed it over to the Navy as a hospital for disabled sailors. Greenwich is now a Royal Naval College.

It Happened Here

Duke Humphrey created the first great library in Britain at Greenwich.

It was probably the first palace in Britain to have glass in the windows. This was installed by Margaret, wife of Henry VI.

Princess Victoria and Prince Albert, when children, in the gardens at Kensington. Kensington Palace was where Queen Victoria lived with her mother before her accession to the throne. The palace is still a royal home. It is used nowadays by junior members of the Royal Family.

Under the Tudors, Greenwich was the scene of magnificent water carnivals on the Thames. Henry VIII would ride out in a gilded vessel, dressed in cloth of gold, and blowing a golden whistle to show he was head of the Navy.

HAMPTON COURT

Like Whitehall, the palace at Hampton Court was built as an extravagance by Archbishop Wolsey. It was so magnificent that it ended up in the hands of Henry VIII. It was a retreat, not only for succeeding Monarchs but also for Oliver Cromwell. It never became as large as Whitehall or Westminster.

Under George III, the palace was converted into "Grace and Favour" apartments (members of the royal household were given rent-free, life-time tenancy in return for long and loyal service). Many of these apartments survive today on the same basis.

It Happened Here

During Mass at Hampton Court, Cranmer put a note into Henry VIII's hand giving details of the love life of the fifth Queen, Katherine Howard. She was executed.

Mary I honeymooned here with Philip of Spain. It was to prove one of the few happy times in her life.

George II boxed the ears of his grandson, George III, so hard that it is said the boy never wanted to go there again.

KENSINGTON

William III disliked the palace of Whitehall because it was damp and he suffered from asthma. He decided that Nottingham House in Kensington would be a healthier site; and the house was quickly enlarged.

Both William and Queen Anne were keen gardeners, and the area around the palace, which was described as an unsightly gravel pit, was transformed into a magnificent, twenty-six-acre garden. Anne added a "stately Green House" where she loved to grow exotic plants. She also used it for parties.

After the death of George II, Kensington became the home of junior members of the Royal Family — notably, of Queen Victoria's parents, the Duke and Duchess of Kent. It still has the same use.

It Happened Here

Queen Anne had her final quarrel with the Duchess of Marlborough at Kensington. When the Duchess tried to air her grievances, the Queen simply replied, "You said you desire no answer and I shall give you none." They never met again.

Anne's husband died here. He was so fat that the Queen ordered "a great many yeomen of the guard to carry the Prince's dear body." She was afraid they might drop him, the stairs being "steep and slippery".

George II joined the family circle in the gallery and "snubbed the Queen, who was drinking chocolate, for being always stuffing, the Princess Emily for not hearing him, the Princess Caroline for being grown fat, the Duke of Cumberland for standing awkwardly."

Early one morning, the young Victoria was still in her dressing gown and slippers when she was told she was Queen.

Henry VIII. Polly, 9

Henry VIII (left), was one of the greatest builder kings in history. The palace of Hampton Court (below). It was here that Charles I quarrelled with his Queen about her extensive French retinue.

BRIGHTON PAVILION

Brighton Pavilion, the last palace to be built in Britain, is quite unlike any other. It is an oriental-style building, created by George IV. The banqueting hall was painted like an eastern sky; and from the claws of a dragon hung a chandelier weighing a tonne. The walls of George's own rooms were covered with pictures of dragons and lotus blossoms. The roof had so many domes, pinnacles, turrets and minarets that someone said it was as if the dome of St Paul's had come to Brighton and had puppies.

Victoria did not care for it and the palace was sold to the town of Brighton for £50,000.

It Happened Here

Mrs Fitzherbert was installed at Brighton Pavilion after her secret marriage to Prince George.

Prince George and his wife welcomed refugees from the French Revolution.

George IV hated signing death warrants, and he wanted Peel to reprieve a murderer. When Peel agreed, George kissed him warmly and gave him one of his own dressing gowns.

Brighton Pavilion, built by George IV, the last palace to be built in Britain.

Present Palaces

Philip won't let the Queen have many palaces because of the dreadfull expense.

Mary, 12, Scottish

The three official palaces are Holyroodhouse, Windsor Castle and Buckingham Palace. The cost of maintaining these buildings is paid by the Government. Sandringham and Balmoral are private homes, where the Royal family spend their holidays. These two are paid for by the Queen, and she would probably agree that they are very expensive to maintain.

HOLYROODHOUSE

There is a legend that David I of Scotland was attacked by the Devil disguised as a mighty stag, while out hunting. The King was wounded; but he managed to clutch a crucifix which, miraculously, appeared between the stag's antlers. The beast vanished and David was left holding the crucifix or rood. In gratitude for his escape, he founded, on the same spot, the Monastery of the Holy Rood.

It is a fact that David I — whatever his reasons — founded the Abbey in 1128. It was a convenient resting place for Scottish kings on their way to and from Edinburgh Castle, and a guest house was added to the Abbey to accommodate visiting royalty.

The guest house expanded. At the end of the fifteenth century, **James IV made Holyrood an official palace.**

Holyroodhouse became the most magnificent royal residence in Scotland, and it was here that succeeding monarchs held court. But in 1603, James VI of Scotland went south to become James I of England. The palace was never to be a regular royal residence again. Much of it was destroyed during the Civil War. The present building was founded by Charles II, but only finished in the reign of George V.

Today, Holyroodhouse is used for a few special occasions in the year. The Queen visits every summer, and a great garden party is held. James V decorated the roof of the original palace with great crowned thistles; and large tubs of thistles — taller than a man — are still a feature at these parties.

Banquets are still held in the Long Gallery, when a dozen pipers march around the table. The Queen is attended by her Royal Company of Archers in green uniforms and black bonnets.

She is also attended by the High Constables who claim to be the oldest police force in the world. Occasionally, on the eve of her departure, there is a Sunset Ceremony when people from

The entrance gates, facing the great tower built by George IV which is the only remaining part of the original palace of Holyroodhouse.

miles around gather in the forecourt to sing "Will ye no come back again?"

It Happened Here

James IV married Margaret, daughter of Henry VII, in 1502. It was known as the wedding of the Thistle and the Rose. Their great-grandson inherited the Crowns of England and Scotland. Their wedding feast was magnificent but guests had to sleep on thirty-five shillings' worth of straw, bought specially for the occasion.

John Knox lectured Mary Queen of Scots on her sins, and reduced her to tears. He reported that her chamber boy could hardly find enough napkins for her to dry her eyes.

Mary's Italian favourite, Rizzio, was dragged from supper with her and murdered. She believed her husband, Darnley, was behind the plot.

Mary danced at the wedding of a servant while the house where her husband lay sick — outside Edinburgh — was blown up.

Charles II, exiled from England, stayed here and, for a time, was accepted as King of Scotland. He had to listen to such long sermons that he took a dislike to the place and never wanted to visit Scotland again!

Bonnie Prince Charlie held court here before his ill-fated invasion of England in 1745. For a few dazzling weeks there was great feasting, dancing and revelry. An onlooker said of the bonnie prince that he looked "a man of fashion but not like a hero or conqueror".

George IV visited in 1822. He was the first King George to come to Scotland. He was also the first King George to wear full Highland dress, with flesh-coloured tights beneath his huge swinging kilt. He admitted "I cannot help smiling at myself".

The palace of Holyroodhouse. The building you
see here was started by Charles II. No British
monarch ever lived here after James VI of
Scotland, later James I of England. The palace
was virtually destroyed during the Civil War and
was rebuilt in the reign of George V.

WINDSOR CASTLE

Many palaces began as royal hideaways and became official royal residences. But the opposite is true of Windsor Castle. It began, like the Tower of London, as a castle; but since it was built, 900 years ago, the soldiers have gone and it has been turned into a royal retreat. The Queen and her family often use the castle for weekends away from London.

William I rented the site of Windsor Castle for twelve shillings a year.

Henry I made his barons swear to accept Matilda as heir to the throne.

King Charles spent his last Christmas in captivity at the castle in 1648.

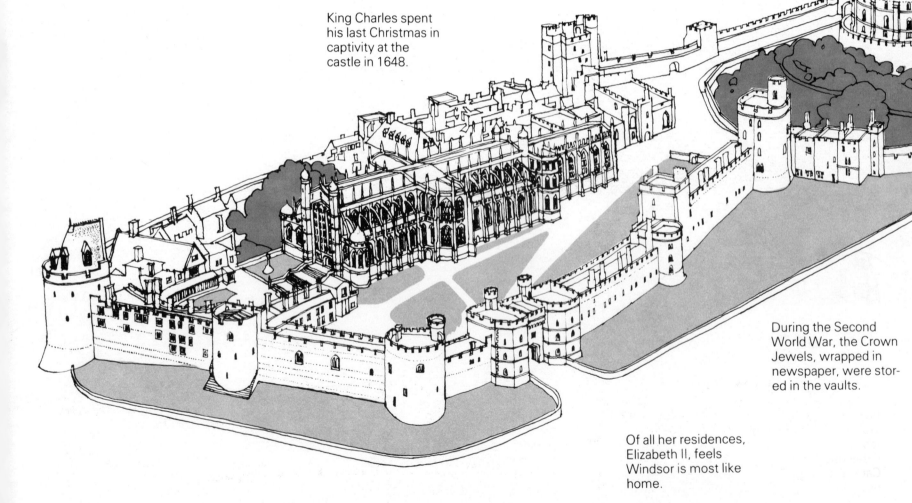

During the Second World War, the Crown Jewels, wrapped in newspaper, were stored in the vaults.

Of all her residences, Elizabeth II, feels Windsor is most like home.

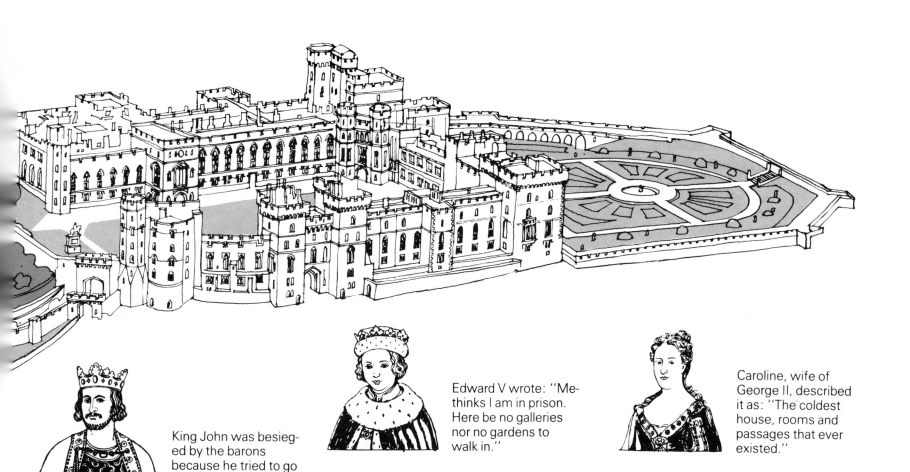

King John was besieged by the barons because he tried to go back on Magna Carta.

Edward V wrote: "Methinks I am in prison. Here be no galleries nor no gardens to walk in."

Caroline, wife of George II, described it as: "The coldest house, rooms and passages that ever existed."

Edward III started work on a great round table, hoping to re-create the glory of Camelot. It was never finished.

Charles II improved the castle and made it more comfortable as a royal home.

George IV spent part of his disastrous honeymoon here.

The first castle was built by William the Conqueror. It was an important link in the great chain of forts that he created to dominate the country he had won by the Battle of Hastings; and the Domesday Book records that he rented the site for twelve shillings a year.

Windsor Castle expanded in much the same way as the Tower of London. It was often used by the Monarch in times of trouble and rebellion; and the fortifications were considered more important than comfort. Henry II replaced the wooden stockade with massive stone walls.

Windsor was also used as a prison, and the dungeons were grim. There are horrible stories of prisoners being locked away and simply left to die of hunger and thirst.

Even in the early days, however, the castle was the scene of many splendid entertainments. The feasts and tournaments, held by Edward I, were famous all over Europe. And it was here that Edward III hoped to re-create the magic of King Arthur's Camelot. Work started on a huge Round Table but it was never finished.

On the whole, Windsor was a popular palace with British Monarchs; but not everyone liked it. The boy king, Edward VI wrote sadly, "Methinks I am in prison. Here be no galleries, nor no gardens to walk in." William III found it altogether too big and grand, and Queen Charlotte, wife of George III, said it was "the coldest house, rooms and passages that ever existed".

An aerial view of Windsor Castle (left). It is one of the Queen's favourite palaces and she spends many weekends there.

The Round Tower at Windsor Castle (right), was built as the keep of the castle by Henry II in the 12th century.

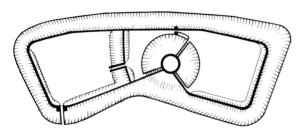

A plan of Windsor Castle. Like the Tower of London, it was more of a fortress than a palace in the early days.

George IV, however, decided to make it the greatest palace in Europe. He spent over a million pounds on improvements and he certainly made it far more magnificent. But certain practical things, like the drains and the cold, remained a problem. Victoria's husband, Albert, died of typhoid, and it is thought that the bad drains at Windsor were responsible.

Windsor is so big, guests have been known to wander for hours, looking for their bedrooms.

The passages are almost as wide as a road. The Grand Corridor is 550 feet long. Yet of her five residences, Windsor Castle is said to be the one that the present queen feels is home.

Maybe this is because she and her sister, Princess Margaret, spent much of their childhood there during the Second World War. This is where they did their lessons, rode their ponies, played with the corgis and waited for their parents to come home from London. This is where they hung up their Christmas stockings and acted in their own Christmas pantomimes. When the air raid sirens sounded, they would run to the great cellars, carrying little suitcases full of their dolls, books and other treasures.

Windsor Castle is the place where the Royal Family spend Christmas, Easter and week-ends away from London. The Queen's work follows her everywhere; and she is often just as busy at the Castle as she is at Buckingham Palace. But it is still a place where the family can invite their friends and relax. Windsor Castle is no longer a fortress but the thick walls guard the Royal Family's privacy.

It Happened Here

Henry I held court at Windsor one Christmas when there was a brawl between the Archbishops of York and Canterbury because they could not agree who should put the Crown on the King's head.

King John was besieged by his barons when he tried to retract the Magna Carta. The Castle took a terrific battering but was not captured.

Under Edward III, 600 oak trees were used to extend the buildings; and one of his stonemasons, Henry le Smythe, is said to have split 156,000 stones.

Richard II said goodbye to his eleven-year-old wife, Isabel, before setting out for Ireland. It is reported that she cried bitterly and begged him not to leave her, and that he kissed her at least ten times.

Henry VI was shocked when a courtier arranged for him to see a dance performed by half-naked young ladies. He quickly turned his back on them. He also advised the pupils at Eton not to visit the court in case they were corrupted by his courtiers.

Henry VIII held a banquet for thirty people. The menu consisted of 800 eggs, 90 dishes of butter, 80 loaves of chestnut bread, 300 wafers of marzipan, 20 pints per person of wine, ale and beer. Each guest was also expected to eat six apples, seven pears and ten oranges. The main courses of beef, veal, lamb, capons, plovers, woodcock, partridges, herons, snipe, leverets and larks' tongues were to follow.

It is not, perhaps, surprising to hear that ropes and pulleys had to be installed to heave fat Henry VIII to bed.

The first performance of Shakespeare's play *The Merry Wives of Windsor* took place at the Castle in front of Elizabeth I. She is said to have commissioned the play.

Elizabeth I was terrified of catching the plague. A gallows was constructed at Windsor, and anyone who came from London during times of plague, who threatened to infect Elizabeth, was hanged without argument.

The King's Beasts at Windsor Castle, originally a heraldic design, they were later used as ornamentation.

James I complained furiously about the poachers and trespassers in Windsor Park. He thought it was outrageous that they stole his game and carried off his wood!

Charles I was imprisoned here. His chief amusement was reading sermons and Shakespeare.

Charles II commissioned many lavish decorations. Allegorical figures were painted on the walls and ceilings; and Charles himself was shown surrounded by the virtues of Temperance, Prudence and Fortitude.

The first Golden Jubilee was celebrated here by the Royal Family. It was rather a sad occasion because the King, George III, was too ill to take part. But there was a party, with a whole roasted ox and a giant plum pudding.

Queen Mary's doll's house at Windsor. It was designed by Lutyens and furnished down to the tiniest detail.

George IV spent the first night of his disastrous honeymoon here. Caroline was later to complain that he forced her to smoke a pipe.

Victoria's mother quarrelled with William IV. He said she had insulted him grossly and continuously.

Victoria remembered how she had to kiss George IV, whom she called her Uncle King. She said it was too disgusting because his face was covered in grease paint.

The French Foreign Minister stayed here with Queeen Victoria. One evening, he failed to find his bedroom, wandered endlessly around and blundered at last into the Queen's bedroom where a maid was brushing Victoria's hair.

Queen Victoria's Maid of Honour thought that evenings at Windsor were terribly dull. She wrote, "The dullness of our evenings is a thing impossible to describe".

Smoking was strictly forbidden by Victoria. Even her most important visitors were obliged to sit in their bedrooms, guiltily blowing their cigar smoke up the chimneys.

Edward VIII delivered his Abdication broadcast from here. It began, "At long last I am able to say a few words of my own."

During the Second World War, the Crown Jewels were kept in the castle vaults, wrapped in old newspaper!

When George VI wished to create an extra bathroom in the royal apartments, he found it possible to carve one out of the thickness of a wall.

During the Second World War, Prince Philip used to come down to see his cousin, Princess Elizabeth. He watched her act in the royal children's pantomime.

When Civil War broke out in 1642, Charles I made no attempt to defend Windsor Castle from the rebellious Parliamentary forces. The castle soon fell into their hands. They seized gold and silver plate from the chapel and kept their horses stabled there. They also used it as a prison for captured royalists.

After Charles I's execution in 1649, his body was returned to the castle and buried in the chapel. The burial took place in silence because the Parliamentary authorities would not allow the funeral service in the Book of Common Prayer to be used.

For many years, no one knew that the tomb of Charles I lay in Windsor Castle.

In King Charles's day, the Sovereign's meals were served with great pomp and ceremony and privileged members of the public were allowed into "The King's Public Dining Room" to watch him eat.

Henry VI founded the famous Eton College not far from Windsor. The school still has close connections with the palace.

The Horse-shoe cloisters at Windsor. These tudor-style cottages house the choristers of St George's Chapel.

An aerial view of Buckingham Palace (left). It began as a country retreat but is now in the centre of London.

An early picture of Buckingham Palace (above). It has changed hands many times but is now the London home of the monarch.

BUCKINGHAM PALACE

Buckingham Palace began as a grove of mulberry trees. James I thought the English should be able to manufacture their own silk; so he planted 30,000 black mulberry trees on the land where the Palace now stands, and imported many silkworms. Unluckily, the silkworms were used to eating the leaves of white mulberry trees so they all died!

The name Buckingham arose when Queen Anne gave the land to an old admirer of hers: the Duke of Buckingham. He built Buckingham House; and this was thought to be the finest private palace in London.

Buckingham House became royal property in the reign of George III. The King bought it for £28,000. This was a bargain price for one of the most beautiful houses in London.

He changed the name to the Queen's House. He wanted it for Queen Charlotte who hated court life at the official palace of St James. In those days the small palace was almost a country retreat, surrounded by meadows, grazing cows and songbirds.

The court, however, would not allow the Royal Family to retreat; and more and more court business followed the King to The Queen's House. George IV decided to make the building much bigger and grander and spent far more money on it than Parliament considered sensible.

Not everyone admired George's improvements. Some people thought the King's House in Pimlico — as it was then called — was not as beautiful as the first Buckingham House.

One foreign visitor said he would not live in it rent-free. William IV seems to have agreed for

29

he tried hard to give the Palace away to the Government. He said it would make a fine new House of Parliament, or a fine new barrack for the guards. But both ideas were turned down.

The Monarch who really liked Buckingham Palace was Victoria. She was delighted to get away from her bossy mother at Kensington Palace. This was the first home that belonged completely to *her* and she enjoyed choosing new furniture, new green silk draperies for her four-poster bed and a new throne. (The upholsterer was told the material mustn't cost more than £1,000.) She found too, that Dashy — her beloved spaniel — settled down very happily in his new surroundings.

Like most Monarchs, however, she decided her palace was too small. More and more royal children were born, and she told the Prime Minister, Sir Robert Peel, that she wanted the Palace enlarged. In the end Parliament voted enough money to Victoria for her to add a new wing.

Victoria's successors have not been so fond of the great London palace. Edward VII said it was like a sepulchre. George V said he would like to pull it down. Edward VIII talked of its dank and musty smell. George VI called it an icebox. Prince Philip called it a museum; and both he and the Queen would have liked to stay on at Clarence House.

Yet one cannot imagine the Queen, or indeed Britain, without Buckingham Palace. The great grey building, with its huge walled garden, is at the heart of the Monarchy.

It is still very much lived in. Children feel, like Christopher Robin, that the head looking out of the window just might belong to a king or queen. Or as one Nigerian boy put it, "I think Buckingham Palace is the only proper palace left in all the world, because it is full of royal things going on and royal people and proper guards, too."

It Happened Here

The Duchess of Buckingham, wife of the Duke who built Buckingham House, was a terrible snob. When she was dying, she made her servants promise not to sit down in her presence until they were sure she was dead.

George III ordered a spectacular new Gold State Coach to celebrate Britain's victories over France. Among the decorations are tritons, symbolising Britain's supremacy of the sea.

Queen Charlotte set up the first Christmas tree in England. She was German; and Christmas trees had been popular for some time in her native country.

Royal plumbing was not very efficient. When Victoria moved in, hardly any of the fifty new lavatories worked and a main sewer sometimes seeped into the kitchen.

Prince Albert decided to re-organize the Royal Household. He was shocked to discover that hundreds of tallow candles were put out every day but never lit. They were then taken and re-sold by one of the servants. It was a perk that had existed since the days when George III used tallow candles to cure his colds. Albert stopped the practice immediately.

Albert also reduced the wages of the housemaids from £45 a year to £12. If they worked well, they were given a raise, to £18!

In 1873, Victoria was persuaded to lend Buckingham Palace to the Shah of Persia when he came on a state visit.

Victoria made it a condition that the Shah left most of his wives behind. But the guests insisted on eating on the floor and whole lambs were roasted under the tables. Many holes were burnt in the carpets. There was even a story that a member of the Shah's staff had been executed with a bowstring and buried in the Palace gardens. Victoria was said to be furious.

Edward VII tried to improve the plumbing. In some dressing rooms he installed three basins: one for washing the hands, one for washing the face and one for cleaning the teeth.

Before one of the big garden parties, the ten-year-old Princess Elizabeth said to her younger sister, Princess Margaret, "If you see someone in a funny hat, you mustn't point at it and laugh."

The wife of an American President visited during the Second World War. She found the Palace very uncomfortable because George VI strictly obeyed the laws on food and fuel rationing. They ate very simply, and the rooms were freezing cold.

In 1940, two bombs fell on the Palace, only yards away from where the King was sitting. One of the policemen outside the gates was impressed because he saw the enemy plane fly straight down the Mall at its target. He told the Queen, "A magnificent piece of bombing, Ma'am, if you'll pardon my saying so."

In 1947 a great wedding party was held for Princess Elizabeth and Philip Mountbatten. Guests included the King and Queen of Denmark, the Kings of Norway, Rumania and Iraq, the King and Queen of Yugoslavia, the Queen of the Hellenes, and Prince Bernhard of the Netherlands.

The Crown Prince and Crown Princess of Sweden and Queen Victoria Eugenie of Spain were also there. Queen Mary, then Queen Mother, noted in her diary, "Saw many old friends. I stood from 9.30 to 12.15 a.m.!!! Not bad for eighty."

A State Landau drawn by two half Cleveland Bays, who are brother and sister and bred by the Queen.

The Phantom VI given to the Queen in 1978 as a Jubilee present by the Society of Motor Manufacturers and Traders.

The Gold State Coach (above) is only used for very great occasions, like Coronations. It was built for George III to celebrate Britain's famous victories over the French. It is 24 feet long, 8 feet 3 inches wide and 12 feet high. It weighs about four tons.

A few days before Elizabeth II's coronation in 1953, the great Crown of St Edward was sent round to the Palace. It weighs over five pounds; and the Queen thought she should practise wearing such a weight before the ceremony. She even wore it while feeding the corgis.

When Winston Churchill retired as Prime Minister in 1955 the Queen asked him if he would like a dukedom. Churchill had thought of becoming the Duke of London, but his son told him the title was too grand.

The Queen has been known to serve hot dogs to American visitors. She has always remembered how much her mother and father enjoyed them when they stayed with President Roosevelt in 1939.

At one time young ladies were presented to the Sovereign each year. But in 1958 the Queen decided that this should be stopped. Instead, she has more garden parties and receptions and a mixture of people, with differing backgrounds and careers, are invited.

SANDRINGHAM

Victoria and Albert worried a lot about their eldest son, Edward. They thought he was too fond of parties and gambling and other kinds of pleasure. They also thought that his own country home would make him settle to a quieter, more respectable life. So in 1861, he bought a large estate in Norfolk which was called Sandringham.

Prince Edward certainly loved his country home; but it did not change his lifestyle the way his parents had hoped. Instead, the quiet estate became a whirl of gaiety. Every Monday and Friday, a train from London would pull into the local station at King's Lynn. It was known as the Prince of Wales Special. The lovely, fashionable ladies and the rich, sporting men would arrive, all ready for some royal entertainment.

Sandringham was — and still is — a great place for shooting. As many as 2,000 birds could be brought down in one day. While the men were busy with their guns, the ladies were busy making themselves beautiful. They would get up and dress very prettily for breakfast, then change for afternoon tea, then change again for the magnificent twelve-course dinner. After dinner, the party would play cards and billiards and dance to the music of a barrel organ.

Things quietened down under George V and George VI. Both Kings enjoyed a much more private family life, and they did not care for parties and lavish entertaining. Like Edward, however, they loved shooting; and they loved Sandringham for the same reason that Elizabeth loves Windsor; this was their childhood home. "Dear old Sandringham," wrote George V, "the place I love better than anywhere else in the world."

George V was always to think of Sandringham as home. George VI also loved Sandringham and wrote, "I have always been happy here."

Sandringham continues to be a wonderful holiday home for the Royal Family. It has always

Sandringham House, seen from the gardens. George V always felt that this house was his real home.

been the place where the royal race horses are bred and the stud has included famous performers, like Persimmon and Diamond Jubilee, who won the Derby and many other races for Edward VII.

Earlier monarchs were always adding to the size and grandeur of their houses; and Edward VII certainly enjoyed enlarging Sandringham. But today the opposite is true. The Queen and Prince Philip have, in fact, demolished 91 of the 361 rooms.

Also, like other stately homes, the house and grounds have been opened to the public. There is a popular museum where you can see the racing shoes of the royal horses, saddles, whips and pictures of famous horses and jockeys. There is a fine collection of Coronation mugs.

BALMORAL

When Victoria and Albert visited Scotland they soon fell in love with the country. They decided that a Scottish home was exactly what they wanted and they went ahead with plans to build themselves a house.

The foundation stone of Balmoral was laid in 1853; and the last great residence to be built by a British Monarch was planned and supervised by the royal couple. If their ghosts walk anywhere, it has to be here, for this was their own creation and even now, over a hundred years later, little except the marmalade-coloured paint that they liked has been changed.

The red and grey tartan, designed for the carpets by Albert, is still there. So is the wall-paper embossed with VRI (Victoria Regina Imperatrix). And so are the mounted rams' heads which were once used for holding snuff. The marble statue of Albert, in full Highland dress, still stands in the entrance hall.

During Victoria's later years, the atmosphere could be gloomy. Ministers dreaded going to Balmoral because the journey was so long and the bedrooms were so uncomfortable. Colonel Ponsonby, private secretary to the Queen, describes a dinner at Balmoral. "Her Majesty, who had a cold, sat between her son, Prince Leopold, who never uttered, and Lord Gainsborough, who was deaf. The prolonged silences were only broken by various types of cough — respectful, deep or gouty."

But the Royal Family's love affair with Scotland continues. With its wild 80,000 acres, this is where the Queen comes nearest to getting away from it all. She loves outdoor life in the Highlands, and does not even seem to mind the rain. The whole family may gather here in the summer for a break which must seem all too brief. Other royal holidays might be changed or cancelled, but the weeks set aside for Balmoral — never!

Balmoral (above), is still one of the best-loved of the Queen's holiday homes. The Royal Family visit every summer.

A royal group at Balmoral (below), taken in 1896. This was one of the first photographs to be taken of royalty.

Living in a Palace

INSIDE A PALACE

There are about a thousand rooms in Buckingham Palace and it's a lovely place for roller skating because the passages are so long.

John, 10. English

There are, in fact, about 600 rooms in Buckingham Palace. Many of them are no more than big cupboards or enclosed passages. Some of the corridors are very long and thickly carpeted. Priceless china and pictures are likely to be found along either side of the corridors; so the royal children have had to do their roller skating in the gardens where there are some ideal paths.

Inside the Palace, there are many things you would not expect to find in someone's home. There is a police station, a telephone exchange, a post office, a sick bay, two firemen on duty, a smithy, and work shops, where electrical, plumbing and furniture repairs are done. There are also many offices for members of the Royal Household. Three staff dining rooms are available: one for senior members, like the Keeper of the Privy Purse and Ladies-in-Waiting; another for junior officials; and a canteen for the domestic staff. Only a few rooms in the Palace are kept for the private use of the Royal Family.

There is only one guest suite. It was much used by Victoria's Belgian uncle, and is still called the Belgian suite.

Buckingham Palace is the London home of the Royal Family. It was bought by the Crown in 1761 for £28,000 and was originally called "The Queen's House". Tourists come from all over the world to watch such traditional ceremonies as the Changing of the Guard and Trooping the Colour. Many glittering processions begin and end at the palace.

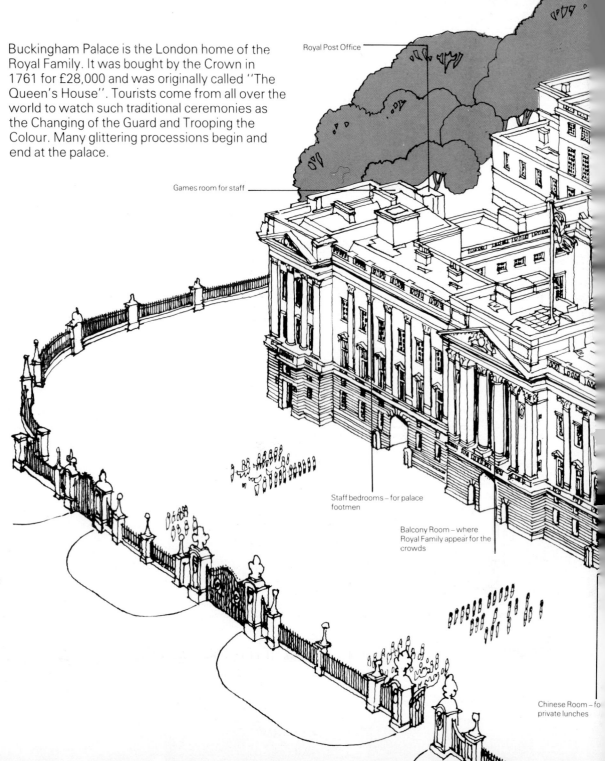

Royal Post Office

Games room for staff

Staff bedrooms – for palace footmen

Balcony Room – where Royal Family appear for the crowds

Chinese Room – fo private lunches

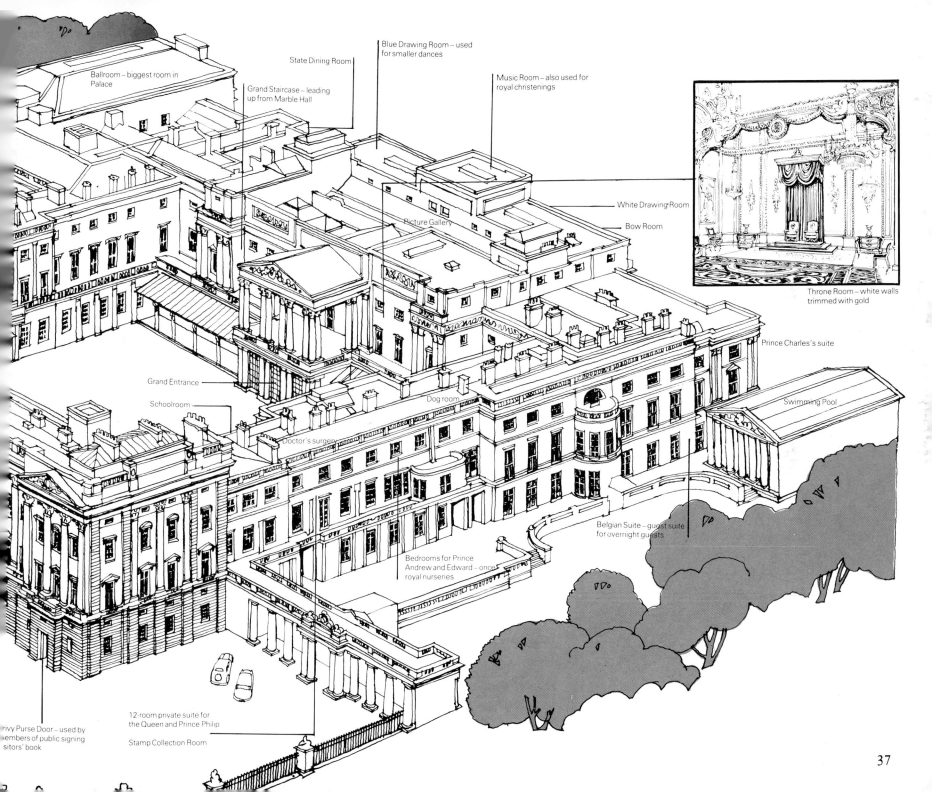

Ballroom – biggest room in Palace

State Dining Room

Grand Staircase – leading up from Marble Hall

Blue Drawing Room – used for smaller dances

Music Room – also used for royal christenings

White Drawing Room

Picture Gallery

Bow Room

Throne Room – white walls trimmed with gold

Prince Charles's suite

Grand Entrance

Schoolroom

Dog room

Swimming Pool

Doctor's surgery

Belgian Suite – guest suite for overnight guests

Bedrooms for Prince Andrew and Edward – once royal nurseries

Privy Purse Door – used by members of public signing visitors' book

12-room private suite for the Queen and Prince Philip

Stamp Collection Room

PRIVATE APARTMENTS

She sleeps in a huge big 4-poster with lovely goldy bobbles on every post.

Elaine, 10. Scottish

The Royal Apartment

Prince Philip calls life in the royal apartments "living over the shop" because so much of the Palace is used for working life. The Queen and Prince Philip live in about a dozen rooms on the first floor; and even here work can still go on.

The Sitting Room

The Queen's sitting room is also used as her study, where she deals with letters, speeches and official documents. The amount of paperwork she has to do every day is enormous. The sitting room is a long room with a high ceiling and a big-bay window, which overlooks the Palace gardens. Beyond the high wall of the garden, which is topped with sharp iron spikes, is Constitution Hill.

This is not a particularly large or grand room. It has a comfortable, lived-in feeling; and one can easily imagine grandchildren or young nephews and nieces playing happily here when they come to visit. The walls and curtains are bluey-green; and the big marble fireplace is surrounded by deep armchairs and a sofa.

Like most mothers, the Queen likes to have a lot of photographs of her children around. There is also a photograph of Prince Philip with a beard. This was taken when he was still a young naval officer. A picture of the Queen herself hangs on one of the walls. It was painted when she was a princess.

The Queen is very fond of flowers, especially carnations, and the room is often full of their scent. She spends a lot of time working at the big Chippendale desk which was once the work desk of her father. But this is also the room where she relaxes, talks on the telephone to her mother and sister, and watches television when she gets the chance.

There is always a bowl of water at the door for the corgis.

The Dining Room

A door opens directly from the central room into the dining room. Again it is not a large room and it is only used for breakfast and informal meals with family and friends. The oval table can be extended to seat ten people.

The Audience Room

The audience room is round the corner from the dining room. It is a formal but very pretty room and it is here that the Queen receives the Prime Minister and other important officials.

The Queen's Bedroom

Although some monarchs have had very big, grand beds (Henry VIII's was 11 feet square) the Queen's bed is a normal size.

Pretty draperies hang from a gilded crown on the bed-head.

The bedroom leads into a dressing room and bathroom. Beyond them are another bathroom, dressing-room and bedroom for Prince Philip.

Prince Philip's Study

Prince Philip's study is more modern in appearance than the other rooms. He has a control panel on his desk so that, without getting up or leaving his chair, he can stop and start his tape recorder, open and shut the curtains and turn his television set around.

Prince Charles' Rooms

These rooms are on the second floor. His study is painted brown and it is rather dark. It overlooks the Mall. (Prince Charles sometimes complains about the noise of the traffic.) His sitting room is blue and crowded with odds and ends. Like his great-grandmother, Queen Mary, Charles is a great collector of treasures; but he is not very good at keeping them tidy. His stereo system is one of the best available.

Charles sleeps in a large, four-poster bed. His bathroom is hung with royal cartoons. The royal nurseries were once on the second floor, but these are now used as bedrooms by Prince Andrew and Prince Edward, when they are at home.

The Queen's Bed. Peter, 12.

A child's impression of the Queen's bed. Many people believe that she sleeps in a four-poster but, in fact, the Queen sleeps in a normal-sized bed.

ROYAL MEWS

Every afternoon on Wednesdays and Thursdays, you will see many people — especially children — waiting to go into the Royal Mews. It is open to the public for two hours on these days. Children love to see the royal horses — the most famous of which are the Windsor Greys. They also love to see the royal harnesses and, of course, the royal carriages including the Gold State coach.

The Gold State coach is like something out of a fairy story. It is very big and richly decorated with golden angels, palm trees, shells and lions' heads. But it is said to be very uncomfortable to ride in. William IV thought it was like a ship in rough sea!

The Glass Coach is the one used for royal weddings. It is called "the Glass Coach" because there are big windows allowing crowds to see the occupants.

In the Middle Ages, the Royal Mews had a different use. Instead of horses and carriages, the King's falcons were kept there while they were changing their plumage. This was called "mewing"; and the word gave rise to the name "Mews". This remains even though the royal falcons have long since disappeared.

The Royal Mews is just around the corner from the Palace, in Buckingham Palace Road. As

A Tandem Cart drawn by two Windsor Greys. The Royal Mews is used to house the Queen's horses and carriages.

well as housing the horses and the carriages, there is also a riding school. This is regularly lent to help disabled children learn to ride. The Royal Family practise here, particularly before occasions like the Trooping of the Colour in honour of the Queen's Official Birthday. It is also the place where the royal cars are garaged.

The most important of the official limousines is the Rolls Royce Phantom, given to the Queen in her Silver Jubilee Year. None of the cars used for official purposes has number plates.

THE STATE ROOMS

The Queen is always giving people lunch and tea and banquets even when she doesn't feel like it and wants to kick off her shoes.

Entertaining has always been part of the royal job. Although other things about the Monarchy have changed, this duty remains the same. Elizabeth II — just like Elizabeth I or even William the Conqueror — has to receive a great many visitors. State rooms are needed if this part of the Monarch's job is to be done properly.

There are, of course, the great State banquets. These are always held in honour of some visiting Head of State, like the King of Saudi Arabia or the President of France; and they take weeks of preparation. The Royal Gold, for instance, has to be cleaned and burnished. (The collection is said to weigh about five tonnes and some of the centre pieces are so heavy, it takes four men to lift them.)

It takes twenty housemaids to clean and polish the vast ballroom where the banquet is held. Hours of work go into the flower arrangements. They stand in the corners of the room, and rise in great banks, up to eight feet tall. Little lights are hidden in the flowers and these are operated by the Palace Steward.

When the lights flash amber, it is the signal for the footmen to take up their positions. When they flash green, it is the signal to start serving a course, or clearing a course away.

Great parties, with 1,600 guests, are held every year for the Diplomatic Corps. And every year, about 30,000 people, from at home and abroad, come to the Buckingham Palace garden parties.

Smaller cocktail parties, lunch parties and dinner parties are constantly held. Prince Philip may be entertaining a Conservation Society; Prince Charles may be entertaining the governors of World College; and the Queen may be giving a party for a foriegn statesman or for a visiting party of Australian politicians. She also entertains ministers from the Government of the day.

Many state rooms are needed at the Palace simply because there are so many state occasions. There is not only the royal entertaining to do. The Queen must also play her part in many official ceremonies.

Every British ambassador going overseas, for example, receives his appointment from her. Every ambassador from another country must be presented to her. Any honour, like a knighthood, a CBE, a George Medal or a Victoria Cross is given by the Queen or by members of the Royal Family.

The Queen has work to do on almost every day of the year. Even when she is on holiday at Sandringham or Balmoral, there is paperwork to deal with and often official visitors to entertain, but Buckingham Palace is the centre of royal ceremonies and much of the royal work is done there. This is why it is run more as a business than a home.

The Marble Hall (below) is part of the Grand Entrance. Visitors to the palace arrive and depart from here.

The Picture Gallery (top right) is a long central corridor which runs through the state rooms. Mirrored glass doors run down either side of the gallery. Many of the Queen's fine pictures are displayed here.

The Ballroom (bottom right) is used for state balls, banquets and investitures. The last ball that was held here was to celebrate Princess Anne's marriage to Captain Mark Phillips. Two thrones stand at one end of the room.

The Music Room (below) is richly decorated with gold and ivory. The ceiling has a gold-encrusted dome and the great chandeliers are the finest in the palace. The room is used for parties and royal christenings.

The Throne Room was used by Queen Victoria for her afternoon Drawing Rooms. It was also used for state investitures, and deputations were received here. Nowadays the Queen is more likely to use the Ballroom on these occasions and the Throne Room is only used for very large parties, photographic sessions and on special occasions, like a Jubilee.

The State Dining Room is used for large dinner parties, but not for State Banquets. The table can be extended to seat up to sixty people. A picture of George IV, in coronation robes, hangs above the fireplace and on either side are portraits of his parents and other Hanoverian royals. Like other rooms in the palace, the ceiling is richly decorated.

The Grand Staircase (left) leads up from the Grand Entrance and the Marble Hall to the Picture Gallery and the main state rooms.

The White Drawing Room (right) is where guests gather for pre-dinner cocktails on large and grand occasions.

A mahogany work table (below) made by William Vile for Queen Charlotte's private apartments at Buckingham House in 1763.

The Belgian Suite (below) is the only big guest suite in the palace. It is named after Victoria's uncle, Leopold of Belgium, a frequent visitor.

The Balcony Room (right) opens on to the big balcony where the Royal Family appear on days of celebration.

A bookcase made for Queen Charlotte and George III by William Vile. It cost £107 14s. George II bought over 67,000 books on every conceivable subject; they filled room after room at Buckingham House.

Peacock
Inachis io

Small Tortoiseshell
Aglais urticae

The Comma
Polygonia c-album

Holly Blue
Celastrina argiolus

Buff-tip Moth
Phalera bucephala

The Palace Gardens

A view across the lake behind Buckingham Palace including a view of the summer house (top left). A close-up of the summer house (bottom far left). The green house, where plants and shrubs for the garden are reared (bottom centre left). Giant rhubarb growing in the gardens of Buckingham Palace (bottom left). Queen Elizabeth the Queen Mother poses under the Waterloo Vase, which was placed in the garden in 1906. The gardens behind Buckingham Palace cover forty acres and contain some marvellous wild life. In 1959 flamingoes were introduced and butterflies abound in the summer. There is also an extensive camomile lawn.

The butterflies illustrated on these pages are only a few of the great variety to be found in the Gardens. It has been estimated that nearly 500 species are here – more than a fifth of all the species in the British Isles.

Red Admiral
Vanessa atalanta

Large White
Pieris brassicae

Small White
Pieris rapae

Vapourer Moth
Orgyia antiqua

Tiger Moth
Arctia caja

A DAY AT THE PALACE

For breakfast the queen likes apple souffle, ham and chops, caviar and a glass of sherry.

The Palace gates are guarded by night as well as by day. Inside the palace, night watchmen move quietly around, making sure that everything is safe. The days when fully armed knights slept outside the door of the Sovereign's bedroom are over; but the Queen's safety remains a matter of great importance.

Terrorists and kidnappers are becoming cleverer and more daring, and a constant watch must be kept on the royal apartments.

The young boy who drew this picture believes that the Queen even has her teeth cleaned for her by the guards!

Guard. Peter, 12.

The telephone exchange must stay open too. If there was some great crisis — if, for example, the United States was attacked — the Queen would be one of the first people to know.

As the day begins, the domestic staff are the first to start work. There are carpets to be vacuumed. Furniture must be polished, and ornaments are dusted. Probably, the staff are glad the State Banquets do not happen very often for on these occasions, the work goes on very late at night and they get little sleep.

Many members of the Queen's Household, however, return to their own homes every evening. The offices of the Ladies in Waiting, the Press Secretaries and the Keeper of the Privy Purse do not get busy until normal working hours begin at around 9 a.m. or later.

The Queen's own day begins about 8 a.m. A footman brings early morning tea to the Royal Apartments, and this is taken to the Queen's bedroom by her dresser, Miss Macdonald. Miss Macdonald also takes in the morning papers and the Queen's private letters. The envelopes are specially initialled to separate them from the rest of the mail. (See pages 112–14 on *Writing to the Queen*.)

When they are dressed, the Queen and Prince Philip have breakfast in the small dining room. Breakfast has been brought up by a footman and it is kept warm on a hotplate. The meal usually consists of eggs and bacon followed by toast and marmalade.

The Queen likes tea with her breakfast. Prince Philip prefers coffee. While the Queen and Prince Philip eat breakfast, bagpipes play outside. Every morning, the Pipe Major, seconded from a Scottish regiment, marches up and down outside the window playing the bagpipes for fifteen minutes. The tradition was started at Balmoral in the time of Victoria and has never been discontinued.

When the royal children were young, breakfast was the time when they ran in from the Palace nurseries to say good morning and there would be half an hour of talk and games. Now everything is quieter (except for the bagpipes) and the Queen may even have time to start on the *Daily Telegraph* crossword puzzle. She often telephones her mother and Princess Margaret at this time.

Most of the Queen's day is taken up with official work. But she may have to choose new dresses or shoes. Perhaps she has to buy a wedding present for a friend, or a birthday present for Princess Anne. Her hair must be done and she may have to go to the oculist or the dentist. There is one big difference between the day-to-day life of the Queen and the life of most other people. The Queen has most things brought to her in the Palace.

There are exceptions. It would be possible to set up a complete dental surgery, and even a complete hospital in the Palace. But the Queen is very practical and does not feel that such a big expense is necessary. So she goes, regularly, to the dentist's. If she needed special medical treatment or an operation, she would probably — like Princess Margaret and Princess Anne — go into hospital.

When she was the mother of young children, the Queen used to spend a lot of time around Christmas in the toy department at Harrods. (So did the young Prince and Princess!) She also enjoyed visits to Fortnum and Mason's and the General Trading Company. There are still presents for young children to be bought — she has nephews, nieces and, of course, grand-children. But nowadays, the Queen finds it hard to find

The Queen as a young mother, walking in the grounds with two of her children, Princess Anne and Prince Andrew.

The Queen with Prince Charles and Princess Anne. When her children were young, the Queen always made time to play with them.

Prince Philip at work at his desk. His study is one of the most modern rooms in the palace today.

time to go shopping herself, and her shopping is done by the Ladies in Waiting.

On the whole, the Queen's private life in London goes on within the walls and gardens of Buckingham Palace. The hairdresser, dress designer, shoemaker, jeweller and so on all come to her. Samples of material for clothes, curtains or upholstery are brought to the Palace. If the Queen wants anything from the shops, it is bought by one of the Ladies in Waiting. Most domestic matters, which have to do with the running of the Palace, can be dealt with when she talks to her Chief Housekeeper or Chef, or the Master of the Household.

The Queen does not have to worry about details like the number of pillowcases or dusters or tins of polish that are needed. But she would be consulted if large sums of money were to be spent on, say, redecorating or replacing curtains and carpets. If a state visitor is expected, she will discuss the arrangements and the menu for the banquet. Most days, however, she hardly has to think about what she will have for dinner as the

Chef sends up his suggestions for meals, the Queen simply ticks the ones she likes, and they are brought to her from the kitchen by a footman.

During a normal day at the Palace, the Queen spends some time on small domestic matters. After breakfast she will discuss with Margaret Macdonald, her dresser, what clothes she will need. (She will probably have to change at least three times during the day for different engagements.) But she will not have to worry about finding or ironing her clothes as they will all be laid out for her. She likes to walk the dogs in the gardens; but mornings are a very busy time and

this is seldom possible until later in the day.

If there is no official lunch, the Queen may eat alone in her private rooms. In London, it is not easy for the Queen to arrange informal family meals because members of her family have so many engagements of their own that they may not be free on the days when she herself is alone. Although the Queen Mother is now in her eighties, she is still a very active royal and undertakes a number of public engagements, though all the Royal Family do their share.

When the Queen lunches alone, or with Prince Philip, they may have a simple meal like cold meat and salad with cheese and biscuits to follow. The Prince likes to drink a glass of beer, but the Queen will probably drink orange squash.

"My granny thinks that all the time
The Queen has things to write and sign.
I expect she reads a lot of books
And talks to footmen and the cooks.
But after lunch my daddy thinks
She's awfully fond of forty winks." Maria, 12.

The Queen does not have much free time; and there are certainly a great many documents and letters for her to read and sign. But she is full of energy and doesn't need an afternoon sleep. If there is a spare half hour after lunch, she is unlikely to put her feet up. Most probably, she will be glad of the chance to get out into the garden with the dogs and walk them round the lake. This may also be a convenient time for her to stop and talk to the gardeners.

As children, the Queen and Princess Margaret had their own gardens to look after. They spent a lot of time digging and weeding and planting; they specially loved to grow polyanthus, tulips, forget-me-nots, Canterbury Bells, Sweet Williams and other colourful flowers. They were also very keen on vegetables; and at one time, Princess Margaret grew five different kinds of potatoes.

Nowadays, though, the Queen is not a working gardener. Her father, George VI, always enjoyed cutting down brambles and making bonfires. Her grandmother, Queen Mary, was specially fond of stripping ivy off trees. But the Queen's day at the Palace does not include occupations like this. She will discuss plans for new trees or shrubs or flower beds; but you are unlikely to find her hoeing or pruning or raking.

If possible, the Queen likes to be back at the Palace in time for tea — a very important meal in her opinion. She may still be on duty and it is quite usual for her to entertain official visitors to a royal cuppa. It is a treat if she can kick off her shoes and relax with Prince Philip or the Queen Mother or Princess Margaret. But even when there are guests, the Queen usually makes the tea herself. The water is boiled in a Victorian silver spirit kettle. It was Prince Philip's idea to convert this to an electric kettle.

The Queen uses her own special blend of Darjeeling tea, kept in a lovely jade tea caddy. Perhaps she will measure out the tea with the silver caddy spoon that was given to her as a wedding present by the nurses and patients of a children's hospital. (They contributed a penny each.) For tea there will be bread and butter, little sandwiches, scones and perhaps crumpets in winter; but the Queen seldom eats rich cakes or fancy biscuits.

When Elizabeth first became Queen, she hardly had a minute to herself. She had been heir to the throne for many years and carefully trained for her work as a future Monarch. But even so, it was a new life and a new job. The first months were bound to be difficult and very very busy. But as a 13-year-old American boy writes: "The Queen and Prince Philip most likely found time

Miss Margaret MacDonald, "Bobo" to the Queen, discussing the Queen's wardrobe with Her Majesty.

The Queen, Lisa. 9.

The Queen enjoys informal family meals with her children. Unfortunately, these are quite rare occasions.

to play with the kids and wallop them sometimes like most normal parents." And it is certainly true that the Queen, even in those first hectic days, made one strict rule. An hour and a half of every evening — from five o'clock to half past six — belonged to the children. And not even the Prime Minister was allowed to interfere with this. Prime Ministers always came to the Palace on Tuesday evenings for an official interview with the Monarch. But the Queen asked Winston Churchill if he would come *after* 6.30p.m. — later than the usual time — so that playtime with Prince Charles and Princess Anne would not be cut short. On nanny's night off, the Queen would also bath the children, read bedtime stories and tuck them up for the night.

Now that all four children are grown up, evenings at the Palace are quieter and emptier. But the dogs are still there; and after tea, she feeds them herself. A footman brings in the dishes containing cooked meats and biscuits and gravy along with the empty dog bowls. With a silver spoon and fork, the Queen mixes a special dinner for each dog.

The Queen hardly ever goes out to official dinners or parties. Only occasionally will she dine informally at a restaurant or slip, secretly, to the theatre or cinema. Her day at the Palace may well end with a quiet dinner with Prince Philip. She may even dine alone, for Prince Philip and Prince Charles feel it is part of their job to accept evening engagements.

Dinner is almost as simple as lunch. Roast lamb and chicken are favourites; so is grilled steak or fish. There are always plenty of vegetables and a side-plate of salad. Instead of dessert, both the Queen and Prince Philip prefer fresh fruit and something savoury — like kidneys rolled in bacon or scrambled egg with anchovies.

They will probably drink a glass of wine.

When she dines alone, the Queen will often eat on a tray in her sitting room, so that she can watch television. Like most people, she loves programmes that make her laugh, and she has a soft spot for *Dad's Army*. She also enjoys *Kojak*, documentary films and the news. Her world, inside the Palace, must often seem far away from the ordinary world of other people. She likes television because this is her best chance to look into ordinary lives beyond the magic, royal circle. Perhaps for the same reason, she often looks through popular magazines in the evening.

This keeps her in touch with everyday life; and it also helps her to know what people think of the Royal Family and the work they do. Probably she would agree with the small boy who said that the Royal Family must get awfully tired of the rubbish that is written about them. But a good Queen must know what is said about her — even if some of the things are unkind or even untrue.

Most of us would love to go to the palace, just to see what it is like. We'd love to be king or queen for a day and find out how different it was from being anyone else. For it *is* different, as you can see; and living in a palace is nothing like living in an ordinary house.

Most people think that it ought to be different: that there is no point having a Queen unless she lives in a royal and very special way. "It's like having a crown," wrote Isabel, aged 11. "You're not a real king or queen unless you have a crown, and you have to live in a palace with guards and gold plates and so on." But it must be remembered, too, that life in a Palace can sometimes be lonely and that the Royal Family cannot be together as much as other families.

There are, of course, times in the year when

they are all on holiday. There are days, even weeks, at Windsor, Sandringham and Balmoral when they enjoy a real family party. It's easy to see why these occasions are so precious to the Queen. But she must also spend many months at Buckingham Palace, and this can be a very different life. She can, of course, talk to close friends and members of her family on the telephone. Prince Charles will drop in for lunch as often as he can. Princess Margaret or the Queen Mother may come to tea. But days may pass when she does not see her mother, her sister, her daughter, her sons or even her husband. This is hard for someone who loves her family and her family life as much as the Queen. But it is not something she would ever complain about. It is simply a part of her job.

Both her father and grandfather, George V and George VI, admitted that it was a relief to get away from their London Palace. They did not find it was really a home; and George VI used to say that he loved Sandringham so much because it was the place where he could forget he was King. In her day at Buckingham Palace, Elizabeth cannot forget she is Queen.

The Queen Feeding Her Dogs. Polly, 9

PEOPLE IN THE PALACE

Seventy pair of servants she have. The footmen are dressed in gold and taller than policemen.

Anouk, 9. Turkish

There are between 300 and 400 full-time members of the Queen's Household. Many more work part-time. On ordinary occasions, the footmen are dressed in black. But there are very fine uniforms for Banquets, designed by George III.

There is a long list of different job titles in the Queen's Household. But many of these titles do not describe the job they would seem to.

The Mistress of the Robes is not in charge of the Queen's wardrobe. The Master of the Horse is not actively in charge of the royal horses and carriages. The Lord Steward has little to do with the domestic staff of the Palace. The Vice Chamberlain is not the deputy of the Lord Chamberlain. The Royal Bargemaster does not command a royal barge.

It might surprise you to learn that the Clerk of the Closet is a bishop who advises the Monarch on religious matters. The Keeper of the Jewel House is also the Governor of the Tower of London, and an Apothecary to the Queen is not a chemist but a doctor.

All these titles are very old. Once upon a time, the Vice Chamberlain was deputy to the Lord Chamberlain, and both were assistants of the Lord Great Chamberlain. The Mistress of the Robes did look after the Queen's wardrobe. (She received the queen's cast-off dresses as one of the perks.) The Master of the Horse was in charge of the royal horses and carriages. The Royal Barge-master and Royal Watermen did run a royal barge on the Thames. The Lord Steward was head of the domestic staff.

But words — like Apothecary or Clerk of the Closet — have changed their meanings as the times have changed. Hundreds of years ago, the easiest road in and out of London was the river Thames. It was used a great deal by early kings.

They sailed between their palaces at Greenwich, Richmond, Westminster and the Tower. Today, roads on land are quicker and easier; and barges have been replaced by cars and helicopters.

Many of the old titles no longer mean a powerful or a full-time job. The Lord Great Chamberlain, the Earl Marshal, the Lord Steward, the Master of the Horse, the Mistress of the Robes continue to attend the Queen at the great ceremonies, but the day-to-day work is done by other people. The Master of the Household runs the Palace in much the same way as the manager would run a grand hotel. The Crown Equerry looks after the royal horses and carriages. The Queen's dresser looks after the Queen's enormous wardrobe which includes more items than can be counted.

The Lord Chamberlain. He sees to the arrangements for most of the state ceremonies, and entertainments; this means a lot of work. Remember 36,000 people come every year just to the garden parties at Buckingham Palace and also to Holyroodhouse. The Lord Chamberlain sends out invitations, decides on the seating arrangements and even — in some cases — what dress should be worn. He also appoints the part-time members of the Household who come

Earl Marshal

Lord Chamberlain

Master of the Hall

Crown Equerry

in to help at these ceremonies. These include **Gentlemen at Arms, Gentlemen Ushers, The Yeomen of the Guard** and the **Royal Company of Archers**.

The Vice Chamberlain. His job has changed completely. He is a member of Parliament and reports on its proceedings to the Queen.

The Lord Chancellor. Another change of job. He is now the head of the Law Lords and does not even report to the Queen. Once he was head of the Monarch's chaplains. In the time of Henry I, his salary was five shillings a day plus an allowance of wine, one thick candle and forty bits of candle.

The Keeper of the Royal Swans. The keeper does indeed keep an eye on the 600 or so swans which live on the Thames. For hundreds of years, swans have belonged to the Monarch; other people could only own the birds with royal permission.

The Poet Laureate. The poet writes poems in honour of the Royal Family. He has an annual salary of £70 a year.

This was fixed in the reign of James I; and though an increase of £27 was allowed by George III, the present Poet Laureate takes the rise in the form of wine from the Queen's wine merchant.

The Master of the Queen's Musick. The master composes music in honour of royal events. He also receives a small salary of £100 a year.

The Surveyors of the Queen's Pictures and Works of Art. They look after the large, extremely valuable, royal collection.

Keeper of the Royal Philatelic Collection. The present Keeper of the royal stamp collection is Mr John Marriott.

Stamp collecting has been a hobby of the Royal Family since 1864, and the collection has grown into several hundred albums. They include nearly all the stamps ever issued in Britain and the Commonwealth. The collection is priceless.

The Lord High Almoner. The Almoner assists the Queen at the great alms-giving ceremony, Royal Maundy when specially minted coins are distributed by the Queen.

Page   Coachman   Footman   Chauffeur   Postillion   Chorister of the Chapels Royal   Master of the Royal Swans

The Kings of Arms, Heralds and Pursuivants

In the old wars, princes found it convenient to have their own banner with their own designs.

This meant they could be easily recognized and followed by their own men in the fighting. It was the beginning of "heraldry", for these designs and pictures came to be known as heraldic emblems and coats of arms. They became part of a family's history (or genealogy). Today the Kings of Arms, Heralds and Pursuivants research the story of old families through the heraldic emblems. They also introduce new peers into the House of Lords, and proclaim a new king or queen.

A Royal Chef, Peter, 12.

A Career in the modern Royal Household

So far, we have been talking about the older titles in the Royal Household. Most of these are now connected with part-time, ceremonial work; and little or no salary goes with them.

But the modern Monarch needs, of course, a modern, full-time staff. Palaces have to be cleaned. Accounts have to be done. Decisions on the Queen's working life have to be taken. The Royal Family have to be protected, by plain clothes detectives as well as by official guards. These workers have to be paid proper salaries — not like the Poet Laureate! The job becomes a career — just like any other.

Can anyone apply for a job in the Royal Household?

You cannot apply to be Lord Great Chamberlain or Earl Marshal because these titles are inherited and can only be held by the members of a certain family. But if you have the right experience, you can apply for other kinds of work.

The royal plumbers, electricians, carpenters, gardeners or grooms may find themselves working in extra grand surroundings. But they are doing the same work as others in their trade. The royal housemaids, laundresses and kitchen staff do much the same job as people employed in a big luxury hotel. They are, however, dealing with very rare and precious things. Accidents can be forgiven at the Hilton Hotel, and it is not the end of the world if a few spoons and forks end up in the dustbin. But if you were Yeoman of the Gold and Silver Pantry or Yeoman of the Glass and China Pantry, it would be a disaster to break or lose anything from the royal collections. Not only is the gold, silver, glass and china very valuable, it is also irreplaceable.

If you wanted to be the Chief Housekeeper (who is in charge of the female domestic staff), the Palace Steward (who is in charge of the male domestic staff) or the Master of the Household (who is in charge of all the staff), you would have to be a very, very good organizer. But the same is true of the senior staff at any large hotel or in any other big business.

Etiquette is not as strict as it was in the old days. Queen Charlotte, wife of George III, would not allow servants to go past a room where she was sitting if the door was open. She insisted they must never knock on a door but always shake the handle. Although the ceremony is not so formal, the staff at Buckingham Palace still behave in a stately way to the Royal Family.

As well as domestic work, there are jobs for typists, telephonists, filing clerks, and secretaries. Again, it is the same work that is done in many other offices.

Even the Keeper of the Privy Purse, who deals with the salaries of the staff, and with the Queen's finances, works in much the same way as other accountants.

Special People

The Ladies in Waiting help to answer the Queen's letter. But they also help to entertain her official and private visitors, attend her official engagements in Britain, accompany her on state visits abroad and they go on holiday with her too. As you can see the work never stops!

If you were a Lady in Waiting, you might find yourself going round a factory, a coal mine or a hospital. Or you might be a guest at the White House in Washington; at Government House in New Zealand; or at the Elysée Palace in France. You might have to talk to the headmaster of a school in the East End of London, to children in an orphanage, or to crippled patients in a

Cheshire Home. You might talk to the wife of an American President, an Arab prince, the Queen of Spain, or the Prime Minister of Great Britain.

The Equerries are gentlemen who attend, like Ladies in Waiting, on the Royal Family. Although the job sounds interesting and at times very glamorous, it can be difficult. You need something of the Queen's own stamina. It is tiring standing around for hours, looking at things which may or may not interest you. In some cases you may have to speak to strangers who can hardly speak the same language. The Queen, or other members of the Royal Family, will be the centre of attention; but you, too, can be noticed. You, too, must learn how to behave when all eyes are upon you.

The Private Secretary to the Queen holds the key position in the Royal Household. The Private Secretary and his assistants are in overall charge of the vast correspondence that passes through the Palace.

The Private Secretary is the link between the Sovereign and the Government — both the Government of Great Britain and of the Commonwealth countries.

He provides, too, the link between the Sovereign and the general public. The Private Secretary is responsible for the Queen's speeches. He is in overall charge of the Press Office, which puts out all statements from the Palace to the press and other media.

All decisions about the Queen's engagements are taken in consultation with the Private Secretary. He is indeed consulted about anything that is of real importance to the Monarchy. In the Second World War, George VI very much wanted to accompany the invasion fleet to Normandy. But his Private Secretary felt, strongly, that this was too dangerous. The King argued; but in the end, he accepted the advice.

The Private Secretary is the right-hand man; yet he remains in the background. In a recent book on the Monarchy, Godfrey Talbot described him as "the least publicised, most self-effacing but most influential of the Silent Men at the Palace".

The Press Secretary is the link between the Palace and the general public. If you have any questions about the Royal Family, it is the Press Secretary, or one of his assistants, who will deal with them.

Again, this is a difficult job. People from all over the world contact the Press Office with requests for all kinds of information. Will the Queen fly to America on Concorde? is Prince Andrew going to get married? how many presents did the Queen Mother receive on her eightieth birthday? There are also many authors, working on books about the Royal Family, who ask for help; and these books cover a wide field. They could be about William I or the six wives of Henry VIII as well as Royalty today.

If you worked in the Press Office, you couldn't possibly carry *all* the answers to *all* the questions in your head. But you would have to know a great deal; and you would be expected to give advice on where information could be found: what books to read, what people to consult and so on.

The Press Office are always ready to help with reasonable questions. But there are certain things which the Royal Family likes to keep private. As Prince Philip once said, this is not because their private lives are particularly strange or secret, but nobody likes to feel that *everything* they do and say is being reported to the whole world.

If you wanted to become a member of the Royal Household, you would have to understand that this privacy is very important. The Press Office is allowed to talk about the Royal Family to the general public; but everyone else who works for the Queen must promise *not to write or talk about their jobs*. It is the same promise you would have to make if you joined the Secret Service.

The Royal Family must be able to trust the people around them — especially the ones who are closest, the ones who know the most. The Queen's dresser, the royal children's nanny, the Pages of the Backstairs (who wait, personally, on the Queen and Prince Philip) could tell tales and write stories that newspapers all over the world would love to buy. They might well be offered large sums of money for such stories. But if the members of the Royal Family are to have any private life, their staff must be trustworthy and the offers must be refused. If you applied for a job in the Palace, your main qualification might be a very simple one. You would have to be *very* discreet.

The Queen and the Yeomen of the Guard. They have been the Monarch's personal bodyguard since the reign of Henry VII.

Royal Records

I wonder which king of England was the fattest?

Nicholas, 8. English

Fattest King
Henry VIII's waistline increased by forty-three centimetres in five years. George IV's waistline measured 140 centimetres — and that was after "much slimming". (World Record: King Taufa'ulatu of Tonga tips the scales at 210 kilos.)

Longest Reign
Victoria reigned for 63 years 216 days. (World Record: Pepi II, a Pharaoh of Egypt, reigned for 94 years.)

Shortest Reign
Lady Jane Grey was Queen for nine days. (World Record: Dauphin Louis Antoine was King of France for fifteen minutes. He then signed the Act of Abdication in favour of Henri V.)

Most Handsome King
Believed to be Edward IV. The Plantagenet Kings were mostly good looking with golden-red hair and blue eyes. Richard III was described as hideous and a hunchback.

He may have been slandered. The Countess of Desmond — who died at the astonishing age of 140 — remembered dancing with Duke Richard and "he was the handsomest man in the room except for this brother, Edward".

Tallest King
Also Edward IV. He measured almost two metres — a gigantic height in those days.

Most Saintly King
Edward the Confessor is the only English king to be canonized. There was talk of making Mary, Queen of Scots, a saint (even though she was suspected of murdering her husband.) But this suggestion came from France.

Bravest King
Richard I, Edward III and Richard III all challenged the head of an enemy army to single combat. This was a noble as well as a brave gesture because the object was to avoid bloodshed. "Two armies," as Edward III told Philip of France, "cannot remain long in the field without producing great destruction. . . it is very desirable to settle the matter briefly to avoid the mortality of Christians." Their challenges were refused.

Cruellest King
Although a hero, Henry V was very ruthless. He besieged Rouen until the inhabitants were so desperate with hunger that they "ete doggys, they ete cattys, they ete mysse, horse and rattys".

Kindest Royal Father
The present Queen would probably claim the record for her father, George VI. He adored his children and treated them with unfailing love and kindness.

Another loving father was Henry III. Even when he suspected that his eldest son (later Edward I) had conspired against him, he said that if they met he would not be able to refrain from kissing his son. The love was returned. Edward heard of his father's death at the same time as the death of one of his own sons. Onlookers were surprised because he grieved more for the old king. But he told them he might have other sons, but never another father.

Harshest Royal Parents
The early Georges hated their eldest sons. George II called his firstborn "the greatest beast in the whole world". His wife, Caroline, was equally harsh. On her deathbed she said of the same son, "At least I have one comfort . . . I shall never see that monster again."

Most Hated Monarch
Mary I was probably the most unpopular. She was the subject of the old nursery rhyme "Mary, Mary, quite contrary".

Meanest King
Henry VII was very careful with his money. He initialled every receipt issued by his Treasurer.

Queen with the Longest Hair
Katherine of Aragon had hair almost down to her feet.

Worst Husband
George I left his wife, Sophia, behind in prison when he came to be King of England. George IV called for brandy after embracing his bride, Caroline. (After a very brief honeymoon, he never lived with her as a husband.) But Henry VIII must take the record. He was the only King who beheaded two wives.

Most Eccentric King

Poor George III had an illness — now curable — which affected his brain. Today he would be perfectly sane; but there was no treatment in his time. So he did many eccentric things — like shaking hands with an oak tree because he thought it was the King of Prussia.

Greatest Animal Lover

The present Queen's love of dogs and horses is famous. She took her corgi, Susan, with her on honeymoon. Another great animal-lover was Queen Alexandra, wife of Edward VII. Once, while sailing up the Nile, she was shown the sheep that was to be cooked for her dinner. She insisted on sending it home to England, alive, for a happy old age.

Gentlest King

Henry VI hated cruelty. At that time, the mangled corpses of traitors were often exposed as a horrible warning. But when Henry saw one he said, "Take it away. I will not have any Christian man so cruelly handled."

He called the boys at Eton College — the school he himself founded — "his young lambs". He told them to be good boys, "gentle and teachable".

Most Sporting Queen

Queen Anne was described as a mighty huntress. Another Queen Anne, wife of James I, was believed to be the best shot with a crossbow.

Most Law-Abiding King

Edward I banished his eldest son from court when he insulted a judge. He also fined himself 20 marks (£13 7s 8d) when he decided that a judgement he had once given was wrong.

Most Modest King

Robert III of Scotland described himself as "the worst of kings and most miserable of men".

Most Loving Husband

King John fell madly in love with a twelve-year-old girl, Isabella. People said that she had cast a spell on him. Henry VIII wrote the most passionate love letters to Anne Boleyn. (They have ended up, rather unexpectedly, in the Vatican Library.) Again, there was talk of witchcraft. Edward VIII was the only King to give up the throne for the woman he loved. For life-long love, it would be hard to beat George VI. It was said that you could always tell by his face whenever Queen Elizabeth came into the room.

> More Royalty was killed in the Tower than in any other place.
>
> Rupert, 11 Australian

Vainest Queen

Elizabeth I had thousands of dresses and was said never to wear the same one twice. As she grew older, her wigs, make-up and ornaments became more extravagant. Elizabeth was so sensitive about her looks that all mirrors were removed from her rooms when she suspected that her beauty was fading.

Most Fastidious King

King John was unusually clean in an age when few others worried about washing. He had a bath twice a month. (A Spanish Queen once said she took a bath once a year, whether she needed it or not!)

Most Scientific King

Charles II made science fashionable. He was fascinated by the behaviour of plants. Also by such odd facts as that ant eggs can sometimes be bigger than ants.

Only Queen to Turn Cartwheels in the Palace

Queen Alexandra, wife of Edward VII.

Most Loving Wife

Victoria mourned the loss of her husband the longest. She would not even attend the wedding of her eldest son, Edward, two years after Albert's death. Queen Elizabeth gave George VI the greatest, most loving support. It was said that he could hardly have taken on the burden of kingship without her by his side.

Most Romantic Queen

Mary Queen of Scots was beautiful, charming and tragic. She became Queen of Scotland at the age of seven days. She was beheaded by her cousin, Elizabeth I, after many years in prison.

Hardest Royal Childhood in Modern Times

Prince Philip was born fifth in line to the throne of Greece. But his family were exiled — with little money. His parents separated and he grew up with rich relations but no real home. He was moved from school to school in France, Britain and Germany. His school clothes were patched and things like bicycles and raincoats were too expensive for him. At his last school, (Gordonstoun, in the North of Scotland) there were runs before breakfast, cold showers, and the boys had to help with heavy building work. Prince Philip helped to build a pigsty. The Prince, who married the future Queen of England, was no sheltered royal. He had had a hard life.

Worst Wife

Isabella, wife of Edward II, helped to depose and murder her husband.

Best Rider

Princess Anne is the only British royal to represent her country riding at the Olympics. She is fearless and determined. Soon after an operation, she worked doggedly to get fit enough for a three-day European Championship — and won it! Shortly after the birth of her son Princess Anne began riding again. She competed in the Badminton Horse Trials five months later.

Busiest Letter Writer

Victoria wrote at least 3,777 letters to her daughter, the Princess Royal.

Most Successful King at the Races

Edward VII's horses won the Derby three times.

RECORDS IN THE PRESENT REIGN

Greatest Number of Royal Guests

In 1980, there were 40,000 guests at the royal garden parties.

Most Fabric in One Dress

Hardy Amies used fifteen metres of tulle in a dress worn by the Queen at the opening of the Sydney Opera House.

Most Receptions

During the Queen's tour of Brazil and Chile, she attended twenty-one evening receptions in twenty-three days.

Most Valuable Brooch

Granny's Chips (see page 110).

The Dress with Most Pearls

Norman Hartnell's wedding dress for the Queen needed 10,000 American pearls.

Most Handshakes

In Washington, the Queen once shook hands with about 2,000 people.

Only Flight in Helicopter

Although the Queen flies many thousands of miles each year, it is considered too dangerous for her to travel by helicopter. The only time she has flown this way was during her visit to Northern Ireland in Jubilee Year. The danger of the helicopter crashing was thought to be less than the danger of a sniper's bullet hitting the Queen during a car procession.

The biggest palace belonged to king Arthur because he had so many knights.

Mark, 10. Welsh

ROYAL QUOTES

"No more mint sauce from my garden. It means deading the lambs."
(Elizabeth II, when a young Princess)

"In life I loved her dearly, nor can I cease to love her in death."
(Edward I, of his wife Eleanor)

"I have very few clothes and have to make them all myself."
(Alexandra, before her marriage to Edward VII)

"Odds Fish, I am an ugly fellow."
(Charles II, inspecting his own portrait)

"I glory in the name of England."
(George III)

"When the Bishop was asked about sin, he replied with simple conviction that he was against it. If I am asked today what I think about family life after 25 years of marriage, I can answer with equal simplicity, I'm for it."
(Elizabeth II)

"Peggy's gone to heaven and I expect Jesus is riding on her now."
(Princess Margaret, on the death of her first pony)

"I'm glad we have been bombed. Now I feel I can look the East End in the face."
(Queen Elizabeth, after Buckingham Palace had been bombed during the Second World War.)

"In truth he was a great sinner, but not as great as I have been."
(Mary, Queen of Scots, referring to the thief who was crucified with Jesus)

"I find him very fat and not heff as handsome as his portrait."
(Princess Caroline, referring to George IV)

"It is offensive to me to suppose that I talk to *any* of my Ladies upon public affairs."
(Queen Victoria)

"I forgive you with all my heart for now I hope you will make an end of all my troubles."
(Mary Queen of Scots, to her executioner)

"You can get used to anyone's face in a week."
(Charles II, on the subject of marriage)

"You are the son of our love."
(Charles I, to his eldest son, Charles)

"We were seeing what were the ugliest faces we could make at the nice soldiers."
(Princess Elizabeth)

"I pray to God that my eldest son [Edward VIII] will never marry and have children, and that nothing will come between Bertie and Lilibet and the throne."
(George V)

"You used a knife on me. Now I am going to use one on you."
(George VI, producing a sword from beside his bed. He was about to bestow a knight-hood on his surgeon, James Learmouth)

"Horses have such a pathetic look. I don't know what it is about them that makes them so lovely."
(Princess Elizabeth)

"Well, Prime Minister, here's a pretty kettle of fish."
(Queen Mary, to Mr Baldwin, discussing the abdication of Edward VIII)

"There you go again, Mary. Always furniture, furniture, furniture."
(George V, to Queen Mary)

"Your work is the rent you pay for the room you occupy on earth."
(Elizabeth, Queen Mother)

"Judging by the brightness of the lightness, somebody must think I have something to say."
(Prince Charles, when asked about a romance)

"Horses *must* have a holiday."
(Princess Elizabeth)

"I'm not sure you look *wholly* angelic, Margaret."
(Queen Elizabeth to Princess Margaret, who was going to a fancy dress party dressed as an angel)

"My father was frightened of his mother, I was frightened of my father, and I am damned well going to see to it that my children are frightened of me."
(George V)

If the present Queen's father was the nicest Dad, who was the nastiest?

Lilla, 11,' New Zealand

"All this is nothing to the feast you and I shall partake this day in Paradise."
(Jane Grey, as she watched her husband's head-less body brought back to the Tower)

"Thank God for a good people."
(George VI, to a crowd in a bombed out area of London in wartime)

"It's better than being called Action Man."
(Prince Charles, on being asked by Joe Gormley how he liked being called by the nick-name "Charlie")

"God bless your Majesty and God damn your dogs."
(Gentleman who had been bitten by a dog of Charles II)

"A lot of laughing goes on in this place."
(Member of the Royal Household, referring to the present Queen's family life at the Palace)

"It is the one thing I do well and can be seen to do well."
(Princess Anne, about her riding)

"I am weary of travelling and am resolved to go abroad no more."
(Charles II)

"My words are my own. My actions are my Ministers"
(Charles II)

"I would rather be a chamberer, having the fruition of Your Highness presence, than an Empress away from it."
(Mary I, to her father, Henry VIII)

"Buckingham Palace is really a very cosy place."
(Princess Margaret)

"One marriage leads to another."
(Prince Andrew)

"All my life I have put my country before everything else and I simply cannot change now."
(Queen Mary, wife of George V)

"I just love people."
(Elizabeth, Queen Mother)

"Why are you crying? I am not very bad."
(Mary II, on her deathbed to her husband William)

"I am not a clever man, but if I had not picked up something from all the brains I've met, I would be an idiot."
(George V)

"The word 'must' is not used to princes."
(Elizabeth I)

ROYAL DISASTERS

The King's Champion
When great Coronation Banquets were still held at Westminster Hall, it was the custom for a knight in full armour to ride in, fling down his gauntlet and challenge to a fight any man who disputed the right and title of the new Sovereign. As a rule, the greatest problem for the Champion was to get his horse to back, politely, out of the Hall. At the banquet for George III, the Champion trained his horse very carefully. The great moment came. The trumpets sounded. The Earl Marshall and the Lord High Constable stood ready to bring him in — and the Champion and his horse entered backwards! (The horse had spent so long learning to go backwards that it had almost forgotten how to go forwards!)

Privy Council Disaster
New members of the Privy Council were to be sworn in before Elizabeth II. It is a formal ceremony, when the Minister kneels, Bible in hand. Somehow, they got themselves kneeling on the wrong side of the room and had to crawl, on their hands and knees, to the right position. One Minister, as he crawled, knocked a book off a table. It had to be rescued by the Queen who looked "blackly furious". Later, when he apologized to her, she said the worst part was that she had nearly laughed. (There are probably many times when the Queen looks severe because she is struggling to keep a straight face.)

Funeral Disaster
At George V's funeral, the Royal Crown was fixed to the lid of the coffin for the procession through London to Westminster. The Maltese Cross, on top of the Crown, worked loose and suddenly fell off. There was the Cross, with its great square sapphire and about a hundred diamonds, rolling in the dust. A company Sergeant Major picked it up and stuffed it in his pocket. Edward VIII was heard to say, "Christ! What will happen next?"

Near Disaster for the Koh-i-Noor Diamond
The great gem — now set in the Queen's Consort's Crown — was given to Victoria by the East India Company. It was entrusted to the care of Sir John Lawrence, who simply put it in his waistcoat pocket and forgot all about it for six weeks. When the moment came to make the presentation to Victoria he did not know where the priceless diamond was! Trying to sound casual, Sir John asked his valet if he had come across any piece of glass in his waistcoat pockets. The valet had. The diamond had looked so pretty that he had kept it in a box along with pins, buttons and beads!

Coronation Disasters
When the aged Lord Rolle came to take his Oath of Allegiance to Victoria, he tripped over his robes and tumbled down the steps to the throne. The Prime Minister, Lord Melbourne, looked "very awkward and uncouth, with his coronet cocked over his nose, his robes under his feet and holding the great Sword of State like a butcher".

The Bishop of Durham lost his place in the prayer book and thrust the great Orb, unexpectedly, at Victoria, who nearly dropped it. The Archbishop was, "as usual, confused and puzzled" and "most awkwardly put the Ring on the wrong finger".

A grimmer disaster took place at the Coronation of William I. The Saxons were cheering the new King but the Norman barons, mistaking the cheers for angry threats, fired on the crowd and killed many.

Débutante Disaster
A great number of well-born young ladies were being presented to the new King, Edward VIII. The ceremony took place in Buckingham Palace gardens; and, as the carefully dressed girls queued up to make their curtsey, there was a sudden downpour. They fled, dripping wet. Before this, a photographer had caught the look of "thunderous boredom" on the King's face. The next evening, the photograph was splashed across the pages of many newspapers, and the king was criticised for his bad manners.

RHYMES ABOUT ROYALTY

George the First was always reckoned
Vile — but viler George the Second.
And what mortal ever heard
Any good of George the Third?
Then from Earth the Fourth descended —
God be praised, the Georges ended.
(from *The Atlas* April 1855)

Edward the Confessor
Slept under the dresser.
When that began to pall
He slept in the hall.
(E.C. Bentley)

The Queenie's a meanie when anyone's late.
She doesn't consider it's regal to wait.
(Joanie, aged 12)

Most gracious Queen, we thee implore
To go away and sin no more.
But if that effort is too great
To go away at any rate.
(Epigram on Caroline, wife of George IV)

Lilibet, Lilibet, marry me please.
Your daddy's decided it's quite a good wheeze.
The world is delighted for everyone knows
You've taken a shine to the shape of my nose.
(George, aged 14, imagining how Prince Philip
proposed to Princess Elizabeth)

ROYAL FIRSTS

The first King to own a car was Edward VII. He
bought a two-cylinder, six-horse-power Daimler
in 1900, and was always shouting, "faster! faster!" at the driver. Queen Alexandra, on the
other hand, was always poking the chauffeur
with her parasol as a signal to slow down!

The first King to own a pocket handkerchief was
Richard II.

The first King of the whole of England was
Egbert, King of the West Saxons. He united
England in 829 AD.

The first Queen **known** to **wear** a pair of frilly-
topped silk stockings was Elizabeth I.

The first King to use sacred oil at his Coronation
was Henry IV.

The first King to read a book in bed was said to
be Henry II.

The first member of the Royal Family to fly was
Edward VIII. He and his brothers, the Dukes of
Gloucester and Kent, had a competition to see
who would get a pilot's licence first. Prince
Edward won.

First king to eat a pineapple grown in England was
Charles II.

THOUGHTS ABOUT ROYALTY

"I don't think it's nice to be too nosey about the
Queen's bathroom and other things she doesn't
want us to know about."
(Joyce, aged 12)

"Prince Philip looks under the bed every night
to see if somebody from television is there."
(Pat, aged 11)

I wish I'd gone to school with Prince
Andrew but it's too late now.

Henrietta, 12, English

Henry VIII and His Six Wives, Julie, 9.

61

The Queen's Working Life

> The old queens had a nice time, they could chop off anyone's head and no one said boo to them.
>
> Richard, 11. English

The job of the early kings and queens had been clear: it was to rule the country and to protect it from its enemies. Those enemies might be at home or they might be potential invaders from across the sea.

But the job of a modern Monarch is not nearly as clear. When she was still a very young princess, Elizabeth might even have found it rather puzzling.

On the one hand, she couldn't help noticing that the Royal Family were special and important. Crowds did not look at other little girls, the way they looked at her and Margaret Rose. When other parents came home from abroad, they probably did not bring three tonnes of presents — given by the countries they had visited — for a baby daughter. People talked of

The Queen on an informal royal "walkabout" Whenever she can, the Queen takes the opportunity to meet her subjects.

the king as if he were the grandest person in the land. All the same, there were a lot of things the king could not do any more.

Elizabeth once said that, if she became Queen, she would pass a law forbidding everyone to make animals work on Sundays. But she had to learn that Monarchs could not make laws any more. A law, it was true, did not become a proper law until it was approved by the Monarch. Nor could anyone become Prime Minister until the Monarch asked him or her to form a Government. Parliament itself could not be opened unless the Monarch was there to open it. But the fact is that the Monarch does not have much choice. Elizabeth might have asked: "What happens if I don't like a law that Parliament wants to pass?" The answer would have been that she had to "approve" it all the same. She might think someone would make a very bad Prime Minister; but if he is the leader of the winning political party, she still has to offer him the job. She could never refuse to open Parliament.

There is no quick, simple answer to the question: "What does a Queen do now?" One of the first things Elizabeth had to understand was that waving to crowds from a golden coach, wearing a real crown, travelling in your own train or sailing in your own yacht was only part of the royal job. Terry, aged 12, put it very well when he wrote: "The Queen does a lot of nice things, like looking at soldiers and giving away medals and flying on Concorde. But she has to do boring things too, like reading papers and setting a good example."

The Good Example

For a child, it probably *was* rather boring. Elizabeth was taught that princesses had to

behave particularly well, and that it was specially bad if they did not. Why? Because so many people were interested in the Royal Family and watched them. There were times when thousands of eyes would be looking at her, and perhaps thousands of children would be influenced by what she did.

She could see that her own parents were very careful to set a good example. They even did so when conditions were risky and dangerous. During the War, the King and Queen might have taken their family to a safer country. But this would have been a sign to the whole of Britain that the King thought the war would be lost. Other people sent their children away from danger, but the Queen said, firmly: "The children won't go without me, and I won't go without the King, and the King won't leave England." So the princesses were sent no further than Windsor Castle; and King George and Queen Elizabeth often stayed in London when the bombs were falling. After a raid, they would visit the worst hit areas and tatheir homes and even their families.

Another example they set had to do with family life. Terry, aged 9, wrote: "My granny says the queen wouldn't be such a good queen if she was nasty to her family, but she likes them and takes her mummy tea in bed." As we said in the first section, a good family life was to become a more and more important part of the Monarchy. (Perhaps George I and George II were unpopular because they were horrid to their children. George I even put his wife in prison.) George VI and Elizabeth loved each other and loved their daughters. The Queen follows her parents' good example. It would be a special failure if the Royal Family appeared to be unhappy and divided.

The Queen, complete with overalls and safety helmet, prepares to visit a coal-face 1,800 feet underground during her visit to the Silverwood Colliery in Yorkshire (left).

Queen Elizabeth and Prince Philip view the village of Aberfan during their visit to the disaster area.

The Queen visits St Michael's School in London, where once fees of one penny per week were charged (above).

The Queen with Mrs Thatcher, whom she sees regularly to discuss affairs of state (below).

Public engagements and royal ceremonies

Most people know that the Queen has to attend the great State Ceremonies — like Trooping the Colour and the State Opening of Parliament. They probably know, too, that she confers honours, like a knighthood or a George Medal, at a ceremony called an Investiture. We shall be talking more about these ceremonies in the next section.

The Queen's engagements cover a wide field. The object is for her to get around and see a lot of things which are important in Britain today. She might inspect a very big and expensive project, like the building of Concorde. It might be something much smaller, like a school for handicapped children.

Let's take a look at the pages of her diary in February 1980 to see where she went and what she saw.

February 8th. Attended the laying up of Lord Mountbatten's Garter Banner at St George's Chapel.

February 13th. Opened the Viking Exhibition at the British Museum.

February 14th. Attended reception for the winners of the Queen's awards for Export and Technology.

February 15th. Attended the YWCA's 125th Anniversary Service at Westminster Abbey.

February 20th. Opened the Salvation Army Hostel at Whitechapel.

February 27th. Opened the restored buildings at University College School, Hampstead.

The Queen is, of course, asked to do more things than she can manage. But she and other members of the Royal Family do a lot.

One day, the Queen received two High Commissioners, a new ambassador presented his credentials and she saw a retiring member of her own staff — while Prince Philip made a speech during an industrial tour of the Midlands.

Prince Charles flew to Wales on the same day, to open a new hospital. The Queen Mother was arranging to visit a cattle show in East Anglia. Princess Alice of Gloucester attended a flower festival. The Duke and Duchess of Gloucester were naming a new ship and Princess Alexandra was arranging to visit some almshouses. This

The Queen is greeted by Lady Churchill, her hostess at a dinner party, while Sir Winston Churchill looks on.

was not an unusual day in the life of the Royal Family.

The Queen's public appearances are a tremendously important side to her work. The fact that people, obviously, want to see her: will even stand for hours in a street to glimpse her driving past — this shows that her presence makes a real difference to an occasion, to a project, to the men and women who meet her.

But here is another part of her job which is equally important.

Behind the scenes

The Queen does not govern. But she still has certain rights. The Government has to inform her about everything — even top secret events — that goes on and she still has the right to "warn" and "advise" her Ministers.

When she first became Queen, Elizabeth — aged twenty-five — must have found it rather strange to be able to warn and advise the old, immensely experienced Winston Churchill. But politicians come and go. (Seven Prime Ministers have come and gone in her reign.) The leaders of other countries come and go too. (Five American Presidents have come and gone.) But the Queen stays. On almost every day of her life, she does her homework and reads all the reports, secret and otherwise, that arrive from the Government in the "boxes". It usually takes her about two hours.

Not all the information in the "boxes" is interesting. Edward VIII found his "boxes" so dull, he half gave up the effort. But dull or not, the Queen never misses — not even when she's on holiday in Balmoral, paying a state visit to Australia or in bed with flu.

Her Prime Ministers would agree that she has a firm grip of current events. Harold Macmillan wrote: "She is astonishingly well informed on every detail." Sir Alec Douglas Home said that her experience was "invaluable". Harold Wilson found her exceedingly good at giving advice on Britain's financial problems. (Even though she was never good at mathematics as a child.)

The Queen meets the Kwa Zulu Company of Dancers after a Royal Variety Performance (above). She thoroughly enjoys the different kinds of dances she sees on her Commonwealth tours.

With Mrs Thatcher (right). It is a new experience for the Queen to have to deal with another woman at the head of the Government.

The Queen talks to some young Brownies, (centre). She was enrolled in the Brownies as a young girl by her aunt, the late Princess Royal.

The Queen accepts a bunch of flowers from a little girl (above). Presenting flowers to the Queen is a token of affection. They are given to her by adults and children alike. On her visits, both at home and abroad, the Queen is presented with a variety of presents. She was given an elephant as an anniversary present once!

Planting a tree (left). She does not actually dig the hole, but she scatters earth around the tree once it has been planted.

On Tuesday evenings the Prime Minister comes to call on the Queen. It is not just a ceremony. They really do talk. The Queen really does give her advice. She also presides over regular meetings of the Privy Council: The Privy Council includes a cross-section of Ministers in the Government and she has a chance to talk to them, too. Informal lunch parties are often held at the Palace when she can meet, or become better acquainted with politicians of any party. Heads of big companies, world famous bankers, representatives from the Commonwealth and foreign countries attend these lunch parties, too. (So do people who have nothing to do with government or big business — like the boxer, Henry Cooper or the television personality, Jimmy Savile.) Simply by talking to so many clever and successful people, the Queen keeps learning herself.

Clearly the children have said something very funny to make the Queen laugh.

There is one more thing that politicians respect in the Queen. They find they can trust her in an unusual way. Secret information, passed on to her, stays secret. If they want to talk freely about their own problems (if, say, they want to let off steam about the Foreign Secretary or the Chancellor of the Exchequer) the audience room at the Palace is the safest place to do it. Their own most trusted friends and colleagues may well be keeping diaries and publishing memoirs. But the Queen stays as silent as the grave. She is known to dislike the way some politicians tell all the secrets of their working life — almost as much as she dislikes her own staff telling tales about the Royal Family.

A new job for the monarchy

"In the old days," wrote Barry, aged 13, Australian, "kings only went abroad when they wanted to kill someone." Although there were a few friendly visits, like the Field of the Cloth of Gold meeting between Henry VIII and the King of France, war was certainly the main reason for royal travel. For a long time, the King commanded the army, like Henry V; and as late as George II, the Monarch still led troops into battle.

Things changed in the last century. Victoria and Albert were related to practically every king in Europe; and visits between members of the family became quite common. But they were family visits rather than state occasions.

It was Edward VII who first began to see that royal travel could really help friendly relations between Britain and other countries. He is still remembered as the King who made friends with England's age old enemy, France. George V's visit to India strengthened the bonds between Britain and the Empire; and after George VI's

visit to Canada, it was said that his Queen's smile brought Canada into the Second World War.

The British Empire no longer exists. But without the Monarch, and the Monarch's visits, it is likely that the Commonwealth would not exist either. (See pages 118–21 on the Queen and the Commonwealth.)

Today the Queen is reckoned to be one of the best ambassadors Britain can send abroad. Again, she does her homework. When she visits a country, she really knows about the country and the people who run it. She can talk to her hosts like she talks to her Ministers: with a lot of understanding and experience. General de Gaulle disliked the English and did not listen much to women. He used to tell his wife: "Be silent, Madam, you know nothing." But after sitting next to the Queen at dinner, he admitted that this English woman knew a great deal.

After a royal visit, friendship with Britain becomes warmer, alliances grow stronger, trade gets better. So the Monarch's latest job as ambassador is important; very important indeed.

Adding it all up

The Queen once received a letter from a child asking her if she was perfect. The Queen replied that queens don't pretend to be perfect. All they can say is that they do their best.

The royal work, as you have seen, is long and hard. It will never be easy to say, in just a few words, what effect it has. But perhaps Janie, aged 12, came close to the truth when she wrote: "The Queen has to be a good person and make us feel we are still a proper country like we have been for a long time." After close on thirty years as Queen, Elizabeth would probably agree that the most important part of her work is to be a good representative of Britain.

De Gaulle and the Queen (above). The French President was not in favour of the English, nor did he like women very much. But he had a great respect for Queen Elizabeth.

The Queen visits St Mary's hospital (left), and peeps into the cot of a thirty-six-hour-old baby called Elizabeth Ann.

The Queen and the Grenadier Guards (top left). The Queen is seen inspecting the First Battalion Grenadier Guards at Windsor Castle.

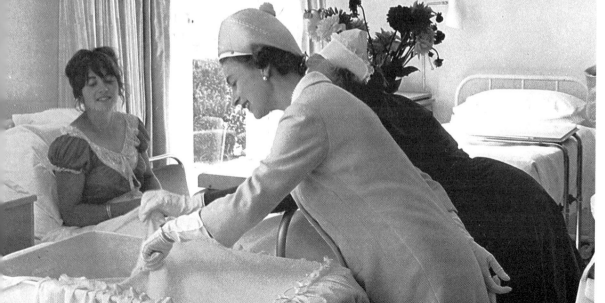

State Ceremonies

Coronations and royal
weddings are more fun than
Disneyland. I guess most
countries can do Disneyland,
but only England the royal
things.

Joe, 14. American

Some of the great royal ceremonies have vanished. Once, the Monarch held great public celebrations at Christmas, Easter and Whitsun when the Crown was worn and alms were distributed. "Touching for the King's Evil" happened regularly. It was believed that the touch of the Sovereign's hand cured certain diseases; and the ceremony was specially popular because the patients also received a gold piece. But William III thought it was a lot of nonsense. When someone begged for the Royal Touch he said, "God give you better health and more sense."

But although these, and many other ceremonies no longer exist, a great number remain. Some are no more than a minor ritual — like "pricking" the appointment of High Sheriffs. Once, when Elizabeth I was sewing in the garden, she was presented with a list of candidates for the office of High Sheriff. Usually, she made a dot with a pen against the chosen names; but — as no pen was handy — she pricked the dot.

Elizabeth II now uses a brass bodkin not a needle when the ceremony to appoint the High Sheriffs takes place.

It is true that the major ceremonies — many with their roots in ancient history, taking weeks of preparation — are done particularly well in Britain. They have been done for so long. It is also true that such ceremonies have died out in other parts of the world along with the old Monarchies.

Some people might consider that these old ceremonies are unnecessary, but as another American boy, aged 15, wrote: "Our Statue of Liberty isn't necessary either, but we don't want to pitch it in the sea."

Certainly they give pleasure. The day may come when nobody comes to watch the Changing of the Guard at Buckingham Palace, nobody fills the street for the Coronation or a Royal Wedding, nobody likes to hear the Royal Salute. But it is hard to believe, isn't it?

The Queen opens Parliament (right). The State Opening of Parliament is one of the most important ceremonies of the year.

Mace

Woolsack

Seal

The Queen takes the salute (above) during the ceremony of Trooping the Colour. This takes place on her official birthday. The plume in her hat depends on the Colour to be trooped that year. White, for instance, is for the Grenadier Guards.

The Queen rides in the procession of foot and mounted soldiers as they march with the Colour towards Buckingham Palace (top right). She takes a final salute at the main Palace gates as the Guards march past.

1st Battalion Grenadier Guards

1st Battalion Irish Guards

1st Battalion Welsh Guards

1st Battalion Scots Guards

2nd Battalion Coldstream Guards

The Colours were the banners used in battle as rallying points for each battalion.

Investitures

Since the days of William I, knighthoods and other honours have been given as a reward for faithful service to the crown. Some kings even sold titles to rich noblemen.

There are many stories about how the name "garter" came to be attached to the Most Noble Order of the Garter. One story has it that a lady lost her blue and gold garter at a dance and Edward III picked it up. When somebody laughed, the King said: "Shame on him who thinks ill of it." (This is still the motto.) Another tale is that the King removed his own garter at the Battle of Crecy and waved it as a signal to attack.

Many titles have come into existence over the centuries. The Most Ancient Order of the Thistle was an honour given by Scottish kings. The Most Honourable Order of the Bath was founded by Henry IV. The Most Distinguished Order of St Michael and St George was founded by William IV. The Most Exalted Order of the Star of India was founded by Victoria. It has not been given to anyone since 1947, and other special honours are given only rarely.

Nowadays, the most usual honours given are Commander of the British Empire, (CBE), Officer or Member of the British Empire, (OBE and MBE), Dame Commander of the British Empire, (DBE). These honours are represented by a medal, and the owner can put the initials — OBE etcetera — after his or her name.

Medals, like the Victoria Cross, are still given for gallantry in war. Others, like the George Medal, for courage in any circumstances (like rescuing someone from a fire or a quicksand). But most honours go to people who have done good work in public services, like politicians or members of local government. Also to musicians, painters, writers, business people and almost anyone who has done good or given pleasure to the country. A few orders — the Garter and the Thistle are among them — remain the personal choice of the Sovereign. But the others are decided by the Prime Minister and his advisers.

About fourteen times a year, the Queen holds an Investiture, usually at Buckingham Palace. Each person who is to receive an honour can bring a few guests. They walk across the red carpet of the Grand Hall, up the Grand Staircase and into the vast cream and gold ballroom. Gilt chairs are set out to seat them. An orchestra plays in a gallery. Just before 11 a.m., five Yeomen of the Guard, resplendent in their gold and scarlet uniforms, enter and stand behind the two great thrones. Then the Queen arrives, everyone stands, and the National Anthem is played. The Lord Chamberlain reads out the

Prince Charles kneels in front of the Queen during his investiture as Prince of Wales and Earl of Chester at Caernarvon Castle in 1969. (right) The Queen knights Francis Chichester after he sailed alone around the world.

name of the first person to be honoured.

If you were to receive a knighthood, you would come forward, bow and kneel on a red stool. The Queen taps you on each shoulder with a sword, but doesn't say the words "Arise, Sir . . ." as people expect. You would then shake her hand, take three steps back and bow again. Medals are hooked on the coat or dress.

The recipient of a medal bows or curtseys, but does not kneel down. The Queen may well say a few words to each person.

Most Noble Order of the Garter (above). Order of the British Empire (right).

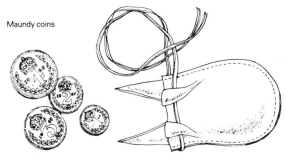
Maundy coins

The Queen and the Dean of Westminster leave Westminster Abbey after the traditional distribution of Royal Maundy.

The Queen and Prince Philip leave St Paul's after the annual "Order of the British Empire" service.

At the end, the Lord Chamberlain steps forward to face the Queen, The National Anthem is played again, the Queen leaves and everyone else disperses. As one recipient said, "It's not just an honour, it's a ceremony you remember all your life."

Royal Maundy

Giving alms to the poor has always been a duty of the Monarch. In the early days, this often took the form of food — probably left-overs from the enormous royal meals — distributed among people waiting at the palace gates. Later, small silver coins were handed out. A half-groat represented 2d, a quarter shilling 3d, and a groat 4d. The most generous handouts came at the great festivals of the Church, like Christmas or Easter.

Royal Maundy is an ancient part of the royal alms-giving. It also goes back to the biblical ceremony when Jesus washed the feet of his disciples on the day before Good Friday (Maundy Thursday). It is recorded that Edward II washed the feet of fifty poor men. Mary I also kissed the feet and gave away her own gown to the poorest woman. The Monarch did not, however, do the most disagreeable part of the work. A laundress, the Sub-Almoner and the Lord High Almoner washed the feet of the poor before the Sovereign, with scented water.

The Monarch stopped taking part in Royal Maundy around 1730. But George V revived the old tradition. The service usually takes place in Westminster Abbey and the Queen always attends. Feet are no longer washed, but the Lord High Almoner and his assistants are still girded with linen towels as a reminder. Nosegays, made up of spring flowers, rosemary and thyme, are presented to the Queen and her attendants. The Queen presents the alms in Tudor style purses of red, white and green. Some of the purses contain ordinary money. But the white purse contains specially minted silver coins.

Trooping the Colour

Regiments of the army, like knights of old, used to display their own banner or "colour" in battle. It helped the men of each regiment to keep together. The Colour was regularly paraded so that the men would be sure to recognize it; and the ceremony was called "Trooping the Colour". The word "trooping" meant "saluted by beat of drum".

This parade first celebrated the birthday of a Monarch in 1805, and the custom has continued ever since. At first, it was held on the king or queen's real birthday; but there were difficulties if the real birthday happened in winter and the weather was bad. So the date is now fixed for a Saturday in June and this has become the official birthday of the Sovereign. The real birthday is celebrated privately.

"Trooping the Colour" involves 1,400 soldiers, about 200 horses and 400 musicians from the royal bands. Each of the royal battalions concerned has its own Colour and they take it in turns to parade in the place of honour.

On the great day, the battalions form up in Horse Guard Parade. The Colour to be trooped has a special escort and is set apart from the others. By 10.50 a.m., everyone is in position and the sound of the Mounted Band of the Household Cavalry is heard approaching. The Royal Procession, all on horseback, appears. The Queen rides side-saddle — probably on a Burmese, a horse she was given by the Royal Canadian Mounted Police. She arrives as the clock strikes 11 a.m. (There was once a man in the clock tower to adjust the hands if necessary.) She takes the salute. The National Anthem is played. She inspects the troops.

Then the Commanding Officer shouts: "Troop!" The bands strike up. The Colour with

The coronation of Queen Elizabeth II (left) in Westminster Abbey in 1953; the first time a coronation was televised. The Royal Family on the balcony of Buckingham Palace (below) after the coronation of the new queen.

74

its escort comes forward. The whole guard present arms, as a salute to the Colour and the National Anthem is played again. The Colour is paraded, slowly, down the ranks. This is the central most solemn part of the ceremony.

The parade is performed with the rhythm and precision of a gigantic dance. The scarlet uniforms of the foot guards add to the brilliance. So do the splendid horses with riders in shining armour, helmets trailing crimson plumes and bright swords held aloft.

The wedding of Princess Anne and Captain Mark Phillips (right), which took place at Westminster Abbey.

Three British queens (far right) await the arrival of the coffin at the funeral of George VI.

When the Queen and her escorts return to the Quadrangle of Buckingham Palace, footmen appear with carrots on silver salvers for the horses.

State opening of Parliament

In January, 1642, Charles I entered the House of Commons with an armed escort. He planned to arrest the five Members who were fighting most actively for the rights of Parliament against the power of the Sovereign. But they had been warned and were not present.

Ever since, the Monarch has not been allowed in the House of Commons. The Queen's speech, which opens a new Parliament, is delivered in the House of Lords.

The Queen drives from Buckingham Palace to the Lords, in the Irish State Coach. Another

coach has already brought the Imperial Crown from the Palace to the Queen's robing room at the Lords; she dons the crimson Robe of State with an ermine lining and an eighteen-foot train.

Four Pages of Honour carry the train as she enters her "parlour" (another name for the House of Lords). She is greeted by the Earl Marshal and the Lord Great Chamberlain, who carries a gold key on his hip. His second title is Keeper of the Palace of Westminster, and this is the key to the Palace.

All the peers and peeresses are in full ceremonial dress. The peeresses wear tiaras. The Queen is installed on a gilded throne and says: "My Lords, pray be seated." Now is the moment when her messenger, called Black Rod, goes to summon the Commons. It is traditional that, as he approaches, the Sergeant at Arms — appear-

ing to fear another Charles I style swoop on the Members — slams the door in his face.

Black Rod knocks three times; the door is opened and the royal summons delivered. "Mr Speaker. The Queen commands the Honourable House to attend Her Majesty immediately in the House of Peers." Again, it is a tradition that the Commons obey the summons rather slowly.

The Queen's Speech has been written by the Prime Minister. It sets out the programme planned by the new Government, and she must get every word right. Nowadays, she wears spectacles to make sure.

Ever since Guy Fawkes attempted to blow up the House of Commons on November 5th, 1605, the Yeomen of the Guard, with pikes and lanterns, make a search. (It was this Guard which caught Guy Fawkes.) Today, police dogs assist.

Coronation

For the last 900 years, this has taken place at Westminster Abbey. It is still much the same service, as the one planned by St Dunstan in 973 AD for the crowning of King Edgar.

Some parts of the ceremony no longer take place. The Abbey service used to be followed by a great banquet in Westminster Hall. The King's Champion, in full armour, would ride into the Hall, trumpets would sound, and anyone who "disputed the right and title of the Sovereign" was challenged to fight. If no challenger appeared, the Monarch drank to his Champion from a gold cup, and handed the cup to him as a present.

Banquets and challenges were stopped in the reign of William IV. So was the Royal Herb Strewer — a lady with six garlanded girls who used to head the Royal Procession strewing sweet herbs and flowers.

The Church Service is long and quite complicated. First, the Archbishop "presented" Elizabeth to the congregation, asking if they would accept her as Queen. A loud "God Save Queen Elizabeth" signified their assent. The Sovereign

The Queen on walkabout during Silver Jubilee Year (left). The Queen and her family on the balcony of the Palace (below).

Prince Charles

Prince Edward   Prince

took the Coronation Oath, promising to keep the peace, repress injustice, and show mercy. She was annointed with holy oil, blessed and consecrated. The Golden Spurs (a symbol of chivalry), the Jewelled Sword, the golden bracelets of sincerity and wisdom (called Armills), the Orb, the Coronation ring, the Glove, the Sceptre and the Rod were presented.

Finally the great Crown of St Edward was raised high by the Archbishop and lowered on to her head. A great shout went up: "God Save the Queen." Trumpets sounded. The guns of the

Tower fired a salute. Elizabeth was now queen indeed.

The Monarch was then enthroned and received homage. Her Consort, Prince Philip, came first to swear allegiance. Next came the Princes of the Blood; then representatives of her other subjects. Another central moment in this deeply religious ceremony was when the Queen received Holy Communion; and, finally, the blessing of the Archbishop.

Accidents do happen at Coronations. Mary I complained that the oil was no longer holy because it had been used on her heretical father. (Elizabeth I merely complained that it smelt revolting!) The Archbishop forced the Coronation ring on to Victoria's wrong finger and she

had to go to bed in it because it would not come off.

At Edward VII's Coronation, the great Crown was nearly put on back to front. (The same problem was to occur at the crowning of George VI.) Some of the holy oil dripped on to Queen Alexandra's nose; and a peeress nearly lost her coronet down the lavatory!

At the rehearsals for George VI's Coronation, Queen Elizabeth got helpless giggles when the photographer vanished beneath a black cloth to take their pictures.

There is a story that, at the same rehearsal, the Great Orb mysteriously disappeared. It was found that six-year-old Princess Margaret was rolling it merrily around in a corner.

The Queen Mother with her grandchildren, Lady Sarah Armstrong Jones and Prince Edward (right).

the late Earl Mountbatten of Burma — Queen Elizabeth II — Prince Philip — Captain Mark Phillips — Princess Anne

Royal Travel

She takes 90 servants and 110 sweetcases

Ella, 9. Arab

The Queen certainly travels. During her Silver Jubilee Year, she flew about 31,000 miles. The whole business of royal travel has had to become streamlined and efficient. It is very unlike the days when 400 carts and 2,400 horses were needed to transport Elizabeth I from one place to another.

Different too, from the travels of Elizabeth's own parents. (Once, when the Queen Mother visited the British Embassy in Paris, it took four men to carry one of her heavy trunks upstairs.)

The Royal Family, like many of the British, have always loved the sea. The first royal yacht was built for Charles II; and perhaps the favourite method of travel for the present Queen and her husband, is on board *Britannia*, the royal yacht.

The Britannia

This was built in the early 1950s at John Brown's Clydebank shipyard at a cost of £2,100,000.

Compared to some of the yachts built for the very rich, the *Britannia* is not extravagant, though it is designed to be a royal home. It is also a place which the Queen can use for entertaining her hosts when she undertakes royal tours abroad.

Saumon Suédoise

Perdreau Rôti Maréchale

Salade

Profiteroles Glacées au Chocolat

Mardi, le 22 février, 1977   Auckland

The Queen and Prince Philip alighting from the Royal Train at Glasgow Central Station on a recent visit. To the right is Mr Stan Butler, the senior Royal Train attendant.

Top row: The insignia found on planes used by the Queen (far left). Some of the aircraft which make up the Queen's Flight (centre). Prince Charles, a fully qualified pilot, takes the controls.

Bottom row: A typical menu from the royal yacht *Britannia*, showing the type of simple food the Queen prefers (far left). The royal yacht *Britannia*, which the Queen and Prince Philip have used to travel all over the world (centre). The Queen enjoys watching the world go by from the deck of the royal yacht.

Special Features

The hull is royal blue. The white superstructure is trimmed with gold. The royal arms are featured on the hull, the royal cypher is on the stern. The yacht is designed to carry a 40-foot barge, a Rolls-Royce or a Land Rover. It used to roll badly but this has been corrected.

Normal crew consists of 21 officers and 256 men. (Pay is no more than for other members of the Navy; but there is strong competition for the jobs.)

There are a few pieces of furniture from earlier royal yachts. (A satinwood desk that belonged to Victoria is in the drawing room.) But most of the furnishings are modern. The royal bedrooms are on the uppermost deck with windows set high so no one can look in. A lift connects them with two studies below. Both have built in desks: Prince Philip's is topped with red leather, the Queen's with green. They also have their own private sitting-out deck.

The sitting room is like something out of a comfortable country house with chintz-covered sofas and chairs. The dining room, which can seat about fifty, is decorated with exotic trophies (like whales' teeth and jewelled daggers) which have been collected on royal travels. Church services take place here. The furniture can be cleared away for receptions of up to 300 guests.)

The yacht is 125.65 metres long. The geared turbine engine, with twin shafts, can produce a speed of 21 knots or about .08 metres a second. Accommodation for the Queen's staff and the crew is very comfortable and convenient; and the whole yacht reflects much of Prince Philip's practical good-sailor sense.

The *Britannia* is not only used as a royal yacht. It takes part in naval exercises; and is also designed for conversion into a hospital ship.

Prince Philip piloting a helicopter on a hectic day when he had to change four times for different engagements, all in different places.

The inside of one of the Queen's state cars is cleaned. The Queen likes music, but not alcohol, in the.cars!

The Queen's Flight

The first member of the Royal Family to fly was Edward VIII. When Prince of Wales, he was taken to the Italian war front in 1918 in a modified Bristol fighter. Later, he owned — and flew himself — De Havilland Moths, a De Havilland Dragon, Dragon Rapides and a Puss Moth.

Flying is indeed a royal hobby. Prince Philip first went solo in 1953, and became a qualified helicopter pilot in 1955. He also once took over the controls of a Hovercraft. Prince Charles is a qualified pilot and Prince Andrew is training as a naval pilot.

The Queen's Flight was first established by Edward VIII. It now consists of three Hawker Siddeley Andovers and two Westland helicopters. They can be recognized by their red, white and blue livery and the royal cypher on the side. Like the *Britannia*, the royal planes are comfortable but not fancy. The royal cabin is painted blue, and there are four reclining seats, copies of magazines are always laid out, and there is an altimeter so the Queen always knows at what height she is travelling.

The royal planes are used for short trips. When the Queen travels long distances overseas, she uses an adapted British Airways or RAF jet-liner. The first thirty rows of seats have been removed and the space used to create a small dining room, a sitting room with divans (that turn into beds for the night) and two small dressing rooms.

The Queen's Flight is also used by Government Ministers and visiting statesmen. The royal planes are financed by the Ministry of Defence. (There is a story that they come under the management of the Master of the Horse, but this is not true!)

Royal Cars

The first royal to own a car was Edward VII. In 1900 he bought a two-cylinder, six-horse-power Daimler; and on his first outing, a groom on horseback rode in front. But it was soon obvious that the horse was holding up the car, and the groom was sent home!

Daimlers continued to be the love of the Royal Family for many years. But the present Queen prefers the Rolls-Royce. For official use, she has two Austin Princesses and five Rolls-Royces — all painted a maroon colour. A silver mascot of St George and the Dragon is transferred from car to car, depending on which she herself is using.

The oldest Rolls dates back to 1948. The newest and grandest was presented to the Queen for her Silver Jubilee in 1977 by the Society of Motor Manufacturers and Traders. The dome and rear roof are transparent so the figures inside can be clearly seen.

Royal Trains

Victoria made her first train journey on June 13th, 1842. She travelled from Paddington to Windsor and reported that she was "quite charmed with it". So she ordered the first Royal Train which was almost a palace on wheels.

Victoria ended up with several Royal Trains; but the present Queen only has one. It is made up of ten coaches. The number used depends on the length of the journey and the size of the party. (When only Prince Philip and his staff are travelling, only one coach is used.) Inside, the coaches reflect the sensible, practical taste of the Queen and her husband.

The Queen on a visit to Papua New Guinea, accompanied by Princess Anne and Captain Mark Phillips.

The Crown Jewels

She wears her crown anywhere but on her head because its too HEAVY

Lynn, 11, New Zealand

Crown Jewels not only mean royal crowns. They mean the whole Royal Regalia — the Sceptre, Orb, Coronation Rings, Spurs, Swords and many other items (fifty-eight in all). Royal Regalia are the emblems, or visible signs, of Royalty. They symbolize the qualities monarchs are supposed to possess: dignity, justice, mercy, courage and so on. They are an important feature at the Coronation because this is when the new monarch swears to maintain such virtues.

The Regalia of early British monarchs was sold off by Oliver Cromwell. Much was melted down, and the whole collection went for £2,647. The Black Prince's Ruby, which was set in the helmet of Henry V, was sold for just £4.

When Charles II came to the throne, there was no Regalia for his Coronation. It all had to be made again by the royal goldsmith, at a cost of £31,978. But in time, a few of the old jewels were recovered — among them, the Black Prince's Ruby and a sapphire believed to come from a ring of Edward the Confessor.

A Nigerian boy, aged 11, thinks the present Queen has "several crowns, one for travelling and one for starting Parliament and perhaps one for going to bed in".

The Imperial State Crown, which is worn by the Monarch as she leaves Westminster Abbey after the coronation and on subsequent state occasions. It was made in 1838 for the coronation of Queen Victoria and is studded with many magnificent gems, including the Black Prince's Ruby. Four large pearls which hang from the crown are said to have belonged to Elizabeth 1.

The Monarch is traditionally crowned with St Edward's Crown. The original crown was broken up in 1649.

The Coronation Rings. There is a tradition that the tighter the ring fits, the longer and more successful the reign.

The King's Orb

Queen Mary II's Orb

The Ampulla

The Anointing Spoon

The Ampulla holds the holy oil which is poured into the Annointing Spoon. Most of the regalia had to be made again for Charles II; but a few items from earlier times survive. The Ampulla and Annointing Spoon are among the oldest, and it is thought they may date back to the coronation of John I.

At the Coronation, the Archbishop presents the Orb to the Monarch and says: "Receive this Orb set under the Cross, and remember that the whole world is subject to the Power and Empire of Christ our Redeemer."

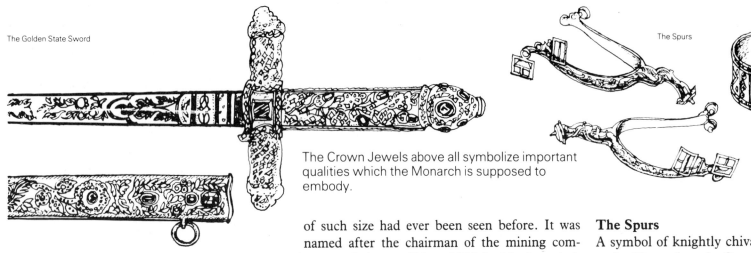

The Golden State Sword

The Spurs

The Bracelets or Armills

The Crown Jewels above all symbolize important qualities which the Monarch is supposed to embody.

The Crown of St Edward

This is the largest crown. One reason it is so big is because it was designed to fit over the great periwig of Charles II. It is certainly a crushing weight for any head, weighing 2.3 kilos. The frame is gold, thickly studded with emeralds, diamonds, rubies and pearls. Victoria — who had a small head and no periwig — was afraid it would fall right down over her face. This disaster did not occur; but another lighter crown, called the Imperial Crown, was made for her. The Crown of St Edward continues to be used at the Coronation; but this is the only occasion when it is worn by the Monarch.

The Imperial Crown

Although lighter, this is by no means short of jewels. There are 2,783 diamonds, 277 pearls, sixteen sapphires, eleven emeralds and four rubies. They include the old jewels mentioned earlier: the Prince's Ruby, St Edward's sapphire and Elizabeth's pearls. Among the diamonds is the Second Star of Africa: a huge gem cut from the famous Cullinan Diamond. (When first discovered, the Cullinan Diamond — 3,025 carats — was thought to be a big piece of glass: nothing

of such size had ever been seen before. It was named after the chairman of the mining company and given to Edward VII for his sixty-sixth birthday. Nine great brilliants and 96 small ones, were cut from it.)

The Imperial Crown is worn for the most important state occasions, like the Opening of Parliament.

The Consort Crown

Made in 1937 for the present Queen Mother. It contains another famous diamond — this time from India — called Koh-i-Noor. There is a legend that it will bring good luck to any woman who wears it, but bad luck to a man.

The Imperial Crown of India

The Crown of St Edward and the Imperial Crown cannot be taken out of Britain. When George V visited India and received the homage of the Indian princes, a new Crown had to be made for him. This only has 170 diamonds.

Ampulla & Spoon

The Ampulla is a golden jug, shaped like an eagle. It contains the holy oil used to anoint a new Sovereign. This is another relic of the old Regalia — possibly dating back to King John.

The Spurs

A symbol of knightly chivalry. When presented to the Monarch at the Coronation, a king touches them with his feet, a queen with her hands.

The Swords

The Jewelled Sword of State is so encrusted with diamonds, one cannot see the gold blade underneath. It is given into the new Monarch's right hand to "do justice and stop the growth of iniquity". The Monarch's own sword is the two handed Sword of State. There are also the Swords of Justice and Mercy.

Armills

Symbols of sincerity. They are bracelets that were made for the Coronation in 1953 — a gift from the Commonwealth countries.

Coronation Rings

With their white diamonds, red rubies and blue sapphires, they look like Union Jacks. These three rings symbolize the dignity of a Monarch.

Orb of England

A golden globe with an amethyst and cross. Symbolizes the domination of the world by Christianity.

Sceptre

The Sceptre with the Cross signifies royal power and justice. (The First Star of Africa, largest of all the Cullinan diamonds, shines in this sceptre.) The Sceptre with the Dove symbolizes mercy.

Mace

A mace began as a fighting weapon, symbolizing the strength of the Sovereign. They have become a symbol of authority.

These and other items of the Royal Regalia are on view at the Tower. The day before the Coronation, they are taken to the Jerusalem Chapel of Westminster and watched over, all night, by the Dean and the Yeomen of the Guard. The escort to Westminster Abbey includes the scholars of Westminster School. (Westminster boys have been given special privileges at royal ceremonies ever since they knelt, publicly, to pray for Charles I on the day of his execution.)

In 1671 there was a famous attempt to steal the Crown Jewels. A Colonel Blood, disguised as a clergyman, managed to get into the Jewel House. Using a heavy mallet, he flattened the great Crown of St. Edward so that it could be concealed under his cloak. The alarm was raised, but Colonel Blood — shouting "stop thief!" — pretended to be one of the guards. He was only caught at the last minute. Mysteriously, he and his accomplices were pardoned. It is thought that Charles II may have been a secret accomplice himself, hoping to share in the sale of the Jewels. The Merry Monarch was always short of money! But it was also said that he admired daring adventurers and may have forgiven the Colonel simply because he liked his nerve.

In 1841, there was another drama. A great fire

broke out in the Tower of London and all the buildings were threatened. The Jewel House was locked, the keys with the Lord Chamberlain — how could the Regalia be rescued? The flames grew worse, the warders looked on helplessly, but in the end, a brave police officer saved the day. He managed to force the bars of the Jewel House apart with a crowbar and squeezed his body through. In spite of the smoke, he was able to pass the Regalia to the warders and it was taken to safety.

Queen Elizabeth II, on the day of her coronation, holding Sceptre and Orb and wearing the Imperial State Crown (left). The arrival of the State Crown for the Opening of Parliament which is attended by the Queen and her family (below).

85

Royal Money

She ought to live like a royal Queen. otherwise there's no use having a Queen.

Elizabeth, 10. English

MONIES COMING IN

The greater part of the royal money comes from:

The Civil List. This is the money paid every year by the Government to meet the expenses incurred by the Monarchy.

At one time, the Monarch paid the army, civil servants and other costs of running the country. But George III proposed a new system. He handed over the revenues from the Crown Estates to the Government. (These included large parts of London, big country estates and holdings in Government securities.) In return, the Government took over the costs of administrating the country. They also agreed to pay a yearly sum to cover the official expenses of the Monarch.

In most respects, this is the system today. The Government pays a certain sum each year for the expenses incurred, in the course of their official duties, by the Royal Family. This is considerably less than the income from the Crown Estates received by the Government. Compared to other public spending, the Civil List is small. For example, the Government spends some £80,000,000 per annum supporting the arts.

Royal Property. Two parts of the Crown Estates were kept by the Royal Family. The Duchy of Lancaster was retained. (One of the Queen's titles is Duke of Lancaster.) Income from this estate is paid directly to the Queen. The money is handled by the Privy Purse.

The Duchy of Cornwall was also retained. Income is paid to the Prince of Wales. No tax is payable: but, instead of tax, Prince Charles returns half of the income to the Government.

Other members of the Royal Family — like Prince Philip and the Queen Mother — receive an allowance from the Civil List for their official expenses. But it is *only* for expenses and is not a salary.

Private estates, like Sandringham and Balmoral, are liable to normal taxes, like rates. Otherwise, the Queen pays no tax. All other members of the Royal Family are taxed normally.

The Queen is a careful shopper. She likes to get value for her money, and is careful about the lasting quality of the goods she buys . . . children's clothes have big hems for letting down – you can see the tell tale lines on some of Princess Anne's winter coats. All the Royal Family's country clothes are worn until they are decently shabby. Perhaps this is because Princess Elizabeth grew up during the war when economy was continuously urged on her.

Dorothy Laird in her book *How The Queen Reigns*

MONIES GOING OUT

The royal cake looks a big one. But the biggest slice simply goes on salaries for the necessary staff.

Another major slice goes on the upkeep of old and beautiful buildings, like Windsor Castle or Holyroodhouse. The money to maintain the official palaces comes from the Department of the Environment. (The private estates are maintained by the Queen.)

Quite a large slice of the money is needed for the upkeep of the royal collection — like pictures, furniture and other treasures.

There are also expenses connected with official entertainment and royal travel. This includes maintenance of the royal yacht and train, and the Queen's Flight.

There is a generous slice of money for charity. The Royal Family are patrons of many good causes; Save the Children Fund, the World Wildlife Fund, the Red Cross and hundreds more.

Pension schemes for the staff take another slice. Also subsidies to members of the Royal Family who do a lot of official work but receive no income from the Civil List.

Compared to the very rich in other countries, the Queen is not extravagant and is constantly looking for ways to save money.

Every Saturday she is given one shilling for pocket money, and of the expenditure of this vast income she neatly enters every single penny in a little book she keeps for the purpose.

Lady Cynthia Asquith, describing the very young Princess Elizabeth's finances in her book
The King's Daughters

Royal Education

Princes used to be too busy fighting to go to school.

Harry, 12, English

In the early days princes, even as young boys, might find themselves commanding an army. Edward III was only fifteen when he led English troops against an invasion from Scotland. Schooling in warfare was a most important part of the royal education.

But as early as the twelfth century, Henry I was to say that an unlettered king was a crowned ass. There were practical reasons why the heir to the throne had to study, and study hard, as well as fight. Monarchs had to negotiate with envoys from foreign countries, and it was an obvious advantage to speak several languages. Latin was vital because this was often used when the king and his visitors had no other language in common.

History and mathematics were important, too. It was felt that a ruler needed to learn from the experiences of his predecessors. The finances of the country were in the hands of the Monarch. Church and royal government were closely involved; and a young prince was certainly expected to study the Scriptures. Nor were social arts like music, and dancing, neglected. The court was the centre of entertainment and a king was expected to take a leading part in the festivities.

The Sixteenth Century

During the Renaissance, in the sixteenth century, the love of learning became a real love. Latin was no longer just a useful second language, it became the gateway to ancient literature. Greek and Hebrew had the same appeal. The effect of the Renaissance on the education of Henry VIII's three children was considerable, for it began to be felt that a sovereign should also be a great scholar.

The Tudor Children

The standard of education achieved by Mary, Elizabeth and Edward was remarkable. Even more remarkable, perhaps were the achievements of their cousin, Lady Jane Grey.

Their education started when they were around the age of three. (Mary could play musical instruments at the age of four.) They probably worked twice as many hours as the average child does today. By the age of ten Edward had written about a hundred essays in Latin and Greek. He could speak Italian, French and Spanish. He was so good at science that he could argue, convincingly, about the origin of comets with a famous Italian mathematician. His memory was so good that he could "recite all the ports, havens and creeks, not within his own realm only, but also in Scotland and likewise in France".

It is perhaps surprising that Mary and Elizabeth were allowed much the same education as their brother. In later years, princesses like the daughters of George III, endlessly embroidered cushions and netted purses. It was even said that

Prayers copied by Elizabeth I (top right). Dolls made by Queen Victoria and a page from her schoolbook (bottom right).

ORATIONI O VERO ME:
ditationi dalle quali la mente
è incitata a patientemente pa:
tire ogni afflittione, et sprezzare
la vana prosperità di questo mõ:
do, et sempre desiderare leterna
beatitudine: raccolte da alcune
sante opere, per la valorosssima,
et humanissima princessa. Cathe
rina reina d'inghilterra, francia
et hibernia. Tradotte per la signo
ra Elizabetta dalla lingua inglese
in vulgare italiano.

the view Religious Botanist Herbs and flowers may, be regaded by some persons as objects of inferior considaxtion in phylosofy; but every thing must, which hath God for its author

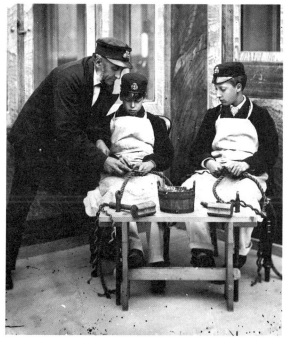

"giving a woman education was like giving a madman a sword". But whatever his other faults as a father, Henry VIII seems to have been proud of his daughters' cleverness and encouraged their learning. Like Edward, they studied the great classical writers in Latin and Greek; and Elizabeth's brilliant knowledge of languages stood her in good stead as Queen. An envoy once read aloud to her an arrogant letter in Latin from the King of Poland. It never occurred to him that a woman would really understand it. But to the delight of her courtiers, Elizabeth at once — and in the most fluent Latin — reprimanded the man for his insolence.

As for Lady Jane Grey she could speak six languages by the time she was six years old. Later, she also taught herself Hebrew and Arabic. When it was observed that her parents preferred sport to reading Plato, she replied: "Alas, good folks, they never felt what pleasure meant."

Another child prodigy was the Tudors' younger cousin, Prince James (later James I). His day began with morning prayers at 5.30 a.m. There would be three hours of Greek before breakfast and three hours of Latin between breakfast and dinner. On top of this, he studied maths, science, geography, zoology, astronomy, rhetoric, logic, French, Italian and magic. At the age of eight, he would lecture visitors on the subject of Knowledge and Ignorance!

There was never any question of sending the royal children to school. A governor (or governess for the girls) would be appointed to take general charge of their education; and various tutors would be brought in to teach special subjects, like French or mathematics. A few carefully selected boys of noble birth would join in some of the lessons with Edward and James; but it is likely that Mary, Elizabeth and Jane worked, for the most part, alone with their tutors. Oddly enough, it seems to have suited them. Victoria complained about her lonely childhood: "I was extremely crushed and kept under." The Tudor children, on the other hand, had nothing but praise and love for their teachers.

There was never to be such a crop of royal scholars again, though one cannot believe the praises sung by all the royal governors and governesses. Lady Elgin, reporting on the daughter of George IV, declared she was "free from all fault whatsoever... perfectly pure and innocent... and that her progress in learning was uncommonly great." This was hardly accurate as the young Princess Charlotte was known to be bone idle, rather stupid and a dreadful liar. However reports on the Tudor children may vary, they *were* prodigies. Elizabeth's tutor, Roger Ascham, even reproached boys because "It is your shame that one maid should go beyond you all in excellency of learning."

Trouble in the Schoolroom

For centuries, the heir to the throne was expected to become the most powerful and important person in the country. Many kings dreamed of educating their heir so perfectly that he or she would become the greatest ruler of all time. Even when the power of the monarchy began to pass into the hands of Parliament, the idea remained that a royal education must be special.

This was reasonable. There is still only one Monarch in Britain. The Monarch's position is

George VI as a student at Oxford (top left). George V and his brother learning to tie knots (bottom left).

The Duke of Windsor in a plane, flying over Windsor Castle (left).

The Princesses Elizabeth and Margaret Rose at work in the schoolroom learning to paint and draw (above).

unlike that of any other man or woman in the country. Special training for such a special job must be needed.

But when the Hanoverian family arrived with George I, it became clear that the royal system of education was not working well. The royal children were giving a great deal of trouble — particularly to their parents.

One reason for this was very simple. Princes and princesses did not work the hours of Edward VI or Jane Grey; but they were still expected to study hard and become good scholars. The fact was, the heirs to the throne were not clever. As a boy, George III was quite a dunce. Far from understanding six languages at the age of six, he could hardly read or write English at the age of eleven. Even so, he was kept at work up to eight hours a day, six days a week — learning subjects which he hated, like Latin and mathematics. One of his tutors said the young prince seemed

to be asleep all day.

A greater educational disaster was Prince Edward, eldest son of Victoria and Albert. The dream persisted that education could make a perfect king; and Albert — who really *was* clever — drew up the most careful plans and chose the most brilliant tutors for his son.

But the little prince was not much good at his lessons. The pressure to *make* him good turned an attractive, sweet-tempered child into a screaming, sometimes violent, little hooligan.

Another problem was the loneliness of the royal schoolroom. It had suited natural scholars, like the Tudor children; but the young Hanoverians were far more boisterous. They liked games and acting and practical jokes. (Even as a man, Prince Frederick — George II's eldest son — thought it was the greatest fun to break other people's windows.) The rough and tumble of a school, with friends of their own choosing,

might have made them happier and less difficult. They might even have been more agreeable to their fathers. (The first Georges rebelled against their parents — but were outraged when their children were troublesome.)

Royal children were only allowed to mix with a few select companions, all aristocratic. Sometimes, as they became older, they were allowed out into the world: the future William IV joined the Navy, but his tutor went too. The Reverend Henry Majendie had to be made an honorary midshipman for the occasion. He sailed with the young prince, supervised his behaviour and continued teaching him the classics.

Albert decided to send Edward to university. But — overdoing it, as usual — he sent him to three, one after the other: Edinburgh, Oxford and Cambridge. Again, there was a lot of supervision, and he was only supposed to dine with senior dons and the clergy. "The more I think of

Princess Elizabeth learns the art of car maintenance (above).
Princess Elizabeth puts her sister's arm in a sling (left).
Princess Elizabeth learns to play the piano (right).

it," wrote Albert, "the more I see the difficulties of the Prince being thrown together with other young men."

The present Queen's own uncle, Edward VIII, talked of his "walled in" childhood; and although he was sent, on his own, to the naval college of Osborne, he was always discouraged by both his parents from mixing with the other boys. George V chose Osborne for Edward because he had been happy in the Navy himself.

But in the end, the British Monarchy has always known how to move with the times. This is one important reason why it has survived. By degrees, a new attitude to the education of royal children began to develop.

The Queen and Princess Margaret

On the face of it, they were educated in the old tradition. They did not go to school but were taught at home by a governess, Miss Crawford ("Crawfie"). She was in overall charge of the schoolroom, and there were teachers for special subjects like music or French.

The princesses joined the Brownies and acted in pantomimes with other children. They were not "walled in" like their Uncle Edward. (Their mother encouraged outside contacts far more than Queen Mary.) Even so, they did not have the chance to mix informally, or make many friends outside the royal circle.

But the attitude of their parents and teachers was not in the old tradition. Perhaps for the first time, it was felt that the system must be made to suit the child not the other way round. The natural talents of the princesses were encouraged; but nobody tried to *make* them different or cleverer children. When it became clear that Elizabeth was not much good at maths, her mother said calmly that she did not think it mattered. (Albert would have laid on extra tutors and recommended punishments.) It was lucky that Elizabeth turned out to be a hard worker and actually enjoyed Latin and English grammar. But she was also allowed to read the books she loved: "Fairy stories, *Alice, Black Beauty, At the Back of the North Wind, Peter Pan,* anything we can find about dogs and horses." (This was how her mother described their reading sessions together.)

Both princesses enjoyed drawing, dancing and music. The dancing teacher, Miss Vacani, said she had never known a pupil pick up a new step as quickly as Elizabeth. The talent was encouraged — just as their natural love of horses and riding was encouraged.

In many ways, it was a successful education. The princesses were happy and did many things they enjoyed. But at the same time, Princess Elizabeth certainly understood the seriousness and specialness of her future work. All the riding and the dancing and the singing did not alter the fact that she was being trained for an unusual and difficult job. One can see today how effective that training has been.

All the same, the differences between royal and normal education remained. Once again,

there were a few carefully selected companions. Once again, the heir to the throne was kept apart. Elizabeth was shy of other children — and later, of other people — simply because she was not used to them. This may be a fact she has regretted.

Prince Philip

Although a royal prince, Philip went to school like other boys and was treated in much the same way. There were no special tutors or privileges. It suited him: every exam he took he passed on his own merits.

The husband of the Queen must have dignity. Like her, he is a centre of public interest. Like her, he must stand a little apart. Philip remains less conventional than some other royals. One cannot imagine George VI advising Britain to pull its finger out, or shouting at photographers to keep their blankety blank cameras further from the Queen. But nobody denies that he has the essential dignity and poise. His more relaxed attitude is refreshing, not out-of-keeping. The fact that he can talk to people easily and naturally, is a positive asset.

"The Queen wanted to keep her children at home and give them lessons herself, but Philip didn't think it was a very good idea." George, 11. South African.

Prince Charles

We don't know what doubts the Queen may have had about sending Charles away to school.

Prince Charles with his younger brother Edward. He has always been fond of children and spends as much time as he can with his nephew, Peter Phillips.

Princess Anne gives away prizes at West Newton School (far right).
Prince Charles arriving at Cheam School in 1957 (right).

But the decision was taken for the first time. The heir to the throne was to have a school education, like that of many other boys in Britain.

There were early lessons for Charles with a governess. (Philip thought there was too much time spent on music and dancing.) But he soon moved on to a day school in London, Hill House. At nine, he went to a boarding school, Cheam, in Hampshire.

To say that he was "just another schoolboy" would not be true. He did not — as one young girl imagined — "bring several footmen and perhaps a handmaiden with him." But he did bring his own detective. Although his lessons, his meals, the games and his bed were the same as those of the other boys, it cannot have been easy for them to behave normally.

Some boys, who wanted to make friends, probably felt shy about making the first advances. Others may have been too pushy and eager. Either way, it was difficult for Charles. Another problem was the tremendous interest taken by newspapers, magazine and television reporters. (During his first 88 days at Cheam, stories about him were published on 68 days.) Some of the boys were even bribed to tell stories and steal his exercise books.

Things became so bad that the Queen and Prince Philip appealed to the reporters. They

Prince Edward on a school outing in Kensington (far right).
Prince Andrew shows his prowess on the hockey field (right)

93

Princess Anne as a Brownie.

said it was proving impossible for Charles to have a normal life at school; and unless things improved, they would have to take him away and educate him privately. By degrees, the publicity died down.

Charles went on to his father's old school in Scotland, Gordonstoun. He spent two terms at a school in Australia, Timbertop; and this was the place where he had his greatest feeling of freedom and informality. He loved it. Trinity College, Cambridge, followed. Then an RAF College where he received his "wings" and according to a report, would have "excelled at high speed aerobatics and would have made an excellent fighter pilot." Afterwards, he followed his father into the Navy.

The younger royal children had an easier time. It was no longer such a novelty to have princes or princesses at school; and Princess Anne settled into a school in Kent called Benenden. Prince Andrew and Prince Edward went to prep school — Heatherdown — and then followed their elder brother to Gordonstoun. Like Charles, Andrew took time out to study in another country; this time, Lakefield College School in Canada. Once again the break seems to have been a great success.

A Success?

The Queen's break with tradition in educating her children at school, and not privately, has undoubtedly been a great success. Although Prince Charles had the hardest time, even he would not want to put the clock back. The old-style schoolroom, with carefully chosen tutors and classmates, is now out of date. Although few people want the heir to the throne to be "just one of the boys" and a Monarch is still expected to behave with dignity, much of his time will be spent meeting and talking to people from many different countries and from all walks of life.

Like his mother, Charles is naturally shy. But his education, unlike hers, helped him to overcome his shyness. Now he can talk with ease and charm to all kinds of people.

The Monarch's role has changed a great deal over the years; fifteen-year-old boys are no longer expected to lead armies into battle. Instead they have become ambassadors and representatives of their countries abroad.

This change is reflected in the way that young princes and princesses are now educated. Today it seems right for royal children to go to school; and this is where, almost certainly, you will find the grandchildren of the Queen.

In future children may find themselves at school with princes and princesses. Princess Anne is determined to give her son, Peter, as normal an education as possible. Any children of Prince Charles, Andrew or Edward may go to day or to boarding school — but school, almost certainly, it will be. The Queen has proved that an ordinary education does not — as Albert or George VI may have feared — make royal children unfit for royal life.

Prince Edward learns to write a letter to his parents (top right).
Prince Charles gets a lesson in shooting a bow and arrow (bottom right).
Prince Andrew in his Cub Scout uniform at Buckingham Palace in 1968 (right).

The young princesses, Elizabeth and Margaret, play Lexicon. Demon Pounce was another favourite of theirs.

The young princess in the garden. Princess Margaret enjoyed growing potatoes more than flowers!

Princess Elizabeth goes for a bicycle ride in the grounds of Windsor Castle in 1942.

Off-Duty

Prince Philip and his sons find it hard to resist a new challenge. Parachute jumps were part of the training in the Navy for Charles and Andrew — but they might have been tempted to try anyway! They have certainly had a go at wind surfing; and Edward has taken a course in conventional gliding. Polo, skiing, swimming, football and other sports have all been popular with the young royals; and as they grow older, many off-duty hours are still spent out-of-doors. Prince Philip loves to drive "four-in-hand" — a racing carriage with four horses.

Princess Elizabeth takes part in a pantomime at Windsor Castle. With her are two other members of the cast.

Princess Elizabeth and a favourite uncle, Louis Mountbatten. Prince Philip took his name when he became a British subject.

Prince Charles rehearses with his fellow students at Trinity College, Cambridge for a forthcoming revue.

The Queen walks along a highland track at Balmoral when she attended the Gun Dog Association's Retriever Trials.

Prince Charles and his cousin, Lady Sarah Armstrong Jones, enjoy a day out in the highlands of Scotland.

Prince Philip stands by the "hide" he has erected in order to enjoy one of his favourite hobbies, birdwatching.

The Queen and Prince Philip enjoy a leisurely stroll through the grounds, while on holiday at Balmoral.

Another of Prince Philip's hobbies is oil painting, which he does whenever he gets the time.

Princess Elizabeth with her father George VI. George was crowned on 12 May, 1937, the day Edward VIII should have been crowned if he had not abdicated to marry Mrs Simpson.

Queen Mary holding her great grandson Prince Charles at his christening.

The Princesses Elizabeth and Margaret with Queen Elizabeth in the grounds of Windsor Castle in 1941.

Princess Anne and Prince Philip relaxing in the grounds of their favourite holiday home, Balmoral.

Prince Edward sailing a small dinghy. Like the rest of his family, the prince thoroughly enjoys outdoor sport.

Prince Charles skiing in Switzerland. The prince has always loved skiing and is very good at the sport.

Prince Charles as a young child in 1952 playing with his toy car in the grounds of Balmoral Castle.

It is not true, as some say, that the Royal Family's only recreations are hunting, shooting and fishing. Prince Philip and the two elder sons share a real love for painting. Both they and the Queen are keen photographers. There is also a lot of musical talent in the family. It is said that Princess Margaret could hum the Merry Widow waltz at the age of eleven months! Though Charles no longer finds time to play his 'cello, he adores listening to music. His favourite composers are Berlioz and Verdi, and they can move the Prince to tears.

Another royal talent is acting. As a boy, it was one of the few things that George III could do well. Princess Margaret has always been called a natural for the stage. Prince Charles was reckoned a good comic actor in revues at Cambridge and charades remain a popular family game.

Royal Animals

The Queen is fond of animals,
Of dogs and swans and horse.
She likes to gallop through the fields
The heather and the gorse.
She really likes to be a queen
A jolly royal, I bet.
But if she couldn't be a Queen
She'd like to be a vet.

Susan, 10. English

The present Queen's love of dogs and horses is well known. But many other monarchs have had the same special affection for animals. Henry I established a zoo at Woodstock. Henry III established another at the Tower. Both Henrys were fascinated by strange beasts from other lands — like elephants, lions, leopards and bears. The animals were even valued above people. It is recorded that the King's leopard was allowed 6d a day for his food, while the Keeper of the leopard only had 1½d!

The faithful dog of Mary Stuart was discovered under her long skirts after her execution.

Princess Elizabeth, aged ten, in the grounds of 145 Piccadilly with a pair of the favourite royal pets – corgis.

(It was a little Skye terrier.) Charles II walked his spaniels as devotedly as the present Queen walks her corgis, and they were allowed in his bedroom. Accounts show "cushions for ye Dogges". He had a tame fox, too, which frightened the Queen when it jumped up unexpectedly onto her bed! Victoria was very devoted to her spaniel, "dear Dashy".

Maybe it was a relief for monarchs to have creatures around which did not know that they were royal, but simply loved them for themselves. Even close members of the family cannot forget the special position of the Sovereign; but animals have no such problems.

Horses

A talent for riding seems to run in the Royal Family. Richard I was a famous horseman. So was Henry VIII — and he kept on riding even when, with his "furnishings", he weighed over thirty-two stone. Charles II could master the most difficult horses at the age of ten. Queen Anne was once known as the "mightiest huntress of her age." George IV loved racing in a carriage and six — a dangerous sport, not unlike Prince Philip and his four-in-hand today. Edward VII bred famous racehorses.

The present Queen and her sister, Margaret, learned to ride on a pony called Peggy. They were taught, partly by their parents (the Queen Mother was an excellent horsewoman) and also by a groom called Owen. Owen thought they were natural riders and they enjoyed themselves so much, they would chatter all the time they rode. He said the only thing that stopped them was a good gallop "and then they jink with laughter".

Many other ponies followed. There were George, Gem, Snowball, Hans, Jock (the Queen said, "Jock taught me more than any other horse,") and the princesses did not just ride. They really helped to look after their horses. The Queen's riding horses are taken with her to Sandringham and Balmoral: she specially loves to ride in Scotland. She's not a competitive rider, like her daughter, but she thinks riding is the nicest way to see the country. She is also interested in breeding and racing. There are around forty brood mares at Sandringham, and the Queen follows the progress of each promising foal very closely and lovingly. She cannot attend all the races where her horses compete, but she arranges for the results to be telephoned to her as soon as possible.

The Queen's children learnt to ride on Shetland ponies; and again, their parents helped to teach them. It was soon clear that Princess Anne had a very unusual talent — and sometimes did unusual things! (She once tried to lead her pony up the steps at Sandringham so that she could ride into the drawing room and surprise her parents.) When she went to school, her pony, High Jinks, went too. Probably her greatest love was the chestnut gelding, Doublet, who took her to victory in the European Three Day Event at Burghley in 1971, when she competed against the pick of international riders.

As a boy, Charles did not have quite the dash and daring of his younger sister. But he is now reckoned to be one of the best polo players in the country. Edward is an excellent rider; and the whole family love to go out together on horseback at Balmoral and Sandringham.

Dogs

The first royal corgi was bought by George VI — then Duke of York — in 1933. It was called Dookie. In 1936 Dookie was joined by another corgi, Jane, who had puppies on Christmas Eve. Two puppies, Crackers and Carol, were kept.

So the princesses grew up with corgis. On her eighteenth birthday, Princess Elizabeth was given her own, Susan. This was a special pet (she even took Susan when she went on honeymoon). When Susan died in 1959, the headstone described her as the "faithful companion of the Queen".

Today, there are seven corgis: Brush, Smoky,

In the grounds of Sandringham House, the small cemetery for the beloved royal corgis, Susan, Sugar and Heather.

The Queen with one of her favourite horses at Balmoral. The Queen loves to ride and takes some of her horses on holiday with her to Scotland. She is also interested in breeding horses and some of the finest horses on the race tracks wear the Queen's colours. All her children have been encouraged to ride and Princess Anne is one of the world's top riders.

Shadow, Jolly, Spark, Myth and Fable, all descended from Susan. An accidental "marriage" between a corgi and one of Princess Margaret's dachshunds resulted in such enchanting puppies that the corgis have now been joined by two "Dorgis", Piper and Chipper. The dogs adore their mistress and follow her almost everywhere. It is said you always know when the Queen is coming because dogs scurry on ahead.

Labradors are another favourite royal breed. George VI introduced yellow labradors into the kennels at Sandringham to be used as shooting dogs. A famous stud dog, Windsor Bob, started the big family that lives there today and which has included many champions. About five bitches are kept for breeding, and all the puppies are named by the Queen. She loves to help train them herself as gun dogs.

OTHER ANIMALS

The Royal Family are sometimes given interesting new pets. Prince Philip was given two pygmy hippopotami by the President of Liberia. Princess Anne was given a brown Syrian bear, Nikki, by the Soviet leaders, Bulganin and Kruschev. The Queen was presented with two jaguars by the Mayor of Brasilia; two beavers, presented by the Hudson Bay Company and two tortoises, given by the Seychelles. A baby crocodile, Mansa, was given to Prince Edward by a village in Gambia. Such pets could not be easily looked after at the Palace and had to be handed over to various zoos.

The largest gift the royal family ever received was a seven-year-old elephant called Jumbo. He was a Silver Wedding present to the Queen. He obviously could not be kept at the Palace and he now lives at Whipsnade zoo.

The Queen with one of her corgis photographed in Buckingham Palace. It is said that you can always tell when the Queen is coming because her dogs come snuffling along ahead! The Queen breeds labradors and trains them herself.

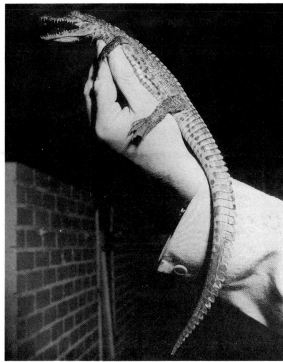

Princess Anne and Florence (far left). The princess plays with her boisterous but affectionate cocker spaniel.

This brown bear, Nikki (left), was a gift from Russia to the Royal Family. The Royal Family receive many animals as gifts from abroad.

The crocodile that slept at Buckingham Palace (above). Mansa was a gift to Prince Andrew from Gambia. He spent his first night at the Palace but now lives at the London Zoo.

Queen Elizabeth riding her horse, Surprise, enters Ascot racecourse (right) during Ascot Week.

Clothes and Jewellery

The Queen in an evening gown wearing jewellery which includes a necklace, bracelets, earings, tiara and Family Orders (far left).

The Queen in a striking yellow evening dress. Her outfits are usually in clear bright colours so that she stands out in a crowd (centre left).

The Queen during her visit to Saudi Arabia (left), in a dress by Hardy Amies. Her wardrobe had to be carefully designed for this visit and most of her dresses had long sleeves and long skirts.

This dress in gold and beige brocade (right) was designed for the Queen to wear on her mother's 80th birthday.

The Queen's Wardrobe

The Queen's job is to be seen. Her clothes are more looked-at than those of any other woman in the world. It is not surprising that her wardrobe takes up three rooms at Buckingham Palace, and that not even her dresser — Margaret Macdonald — could say exactly how many royal dresses are available. All we know is that Norman Hartnell, Hardy Amies and Ian Thomas, the three royal designers, have had to cater for over one thousand occasions.

A few basic points are always kept in mind when designing clothes for the Queen. Colours are crisp and clear: the kind that stand out in a crowd. Hats are kept off the face. Hemlines are "weighted" so a sudden breeze won't blow up the royal skirts. There must never be too many buttons to do up. (Sometimes the Queen has to do some very quick changes.) Shoes must be comfortable rather than high fashion as she has to stand in them for a long time.

The Queen says that, wherever she goes, the weather is always "totally unexpected". This is specially true on state visits abroad when, in the course of a few weeks, she may meet blazing sun, pouring rain, bitter cold and gale force winds. She could be travelling by train, plane, yacht, car, carriage, horse, even by elephant in India; or in a chariot in Borneo pulled by forty men. Somehow, she has to look and dress like a proper Queen; at all times and in all places.

Unlike her sister, Margaret, the Queen is not especially interested in clothes. (As a child she was bored and fidgety at fittings.) But she is too thorough and painstaking to leave everything to

The Queen in a close-fitting hat without a brim so that her face can be clearly seen by people in the crowds.

her designers. Full length designs, in miniature, are submitted to her together with fabric samples. These are carefully studied. She prefers simple styles with no frills or bows. The Queen does not follow the trends of fashion. Princess Anne thought she should try a mini skirt when these were all the rage, but the Queen would not hear of it. "I'm not a filmstar," she says. When an Ascot hat was made for her with a dipping, coquettish brim she ordered it to be straightened out.

She may have fidgeted as a child; but her designers say she is now wonderfully patient at fittings. As every new outfit needs three or four sessions — and she can take up to forty dresses away on a big state visit — that's a lot of fittings to be patient at.

Every design is kept secret. It would not do for other people to be wearing the same clothes at the same time. When Norman Hartnell was designing her wedding dress, he was so afraid cheap copies would be rushed out that he whitewashed the windows of his workroom, locked the sketches in a safe and made his manager sleep on a camp bed beside them.

A frequent question is: "What happens to the Queen's old clothes?" It is likely that her favourite tweeds, tartans and knitwear keep on being worn at Sandringham and Balmoral. The people who know what happens to the rest are not telling.

The Queen's Jewellery

As a teenager, Princess Elizabeth had surprisingly little jewellery of her own. Even at her wedding, the tiara she wore was borrowed from her mother. But she was to inherit, and receive as gifts from other countries, a collection of jewels which may now be the most valuable in all the

Princess Elizabeth leaving Westminster Abbey after her marriage to Prince Philip in 1947 (left). Her beautiful wedding gown was made of white satin, covered with roses and fern fronds worked entirely in pearls and crystal. Seed pearls were used to make the roses and outline the satin petals. A large pearl surrounded with crystal stamens makes the centre of the flower and a pear-shaped pearl lies along each petal. The design for the white satin flowers in the centre of the net panel (above) is the one appliqued onto the net train.

world. (This does not include the Crown Jewels which are considered the property of the State rather than the personal possessions of the Sovereign.)

She owns the pearls of three Queens: the pearls that belonged to Mary Queen of Scots, the pearls of Queen Anne, and the pearls of Queen Caroline (wife of George II). The pearls of the last two Queens are combined in one necklace.

There are emeralds from her grandmother, Queen Mary, aquamarines from Brazil, and diamonds galore from Africa and India — some from the treasure-houses of Indian princes. The greatest diamond in the world, the Cullinan Diamond, was given to Edward VII (see pages 82–5). Although the biggest gems cut from this amazing stone, are set in the Crown Jewels, the smaller "chips" have been made into magnificent brooches, necklaces and rings. These belonged to Queen Mary and Elizabeth still calls them "Granny's chips".

More diamonds came from South Africa, on the Queen's twenty-first birthday; and these she calls "my best diamonds". There is a truly brilliant necklace made up of fifteen large gems; and there are seven more gems in the matching bracelet. From Africa came a beautiful rose-pink diamond, now set in a flower brooch.

The brooch was a personal wedding gift from a Dr Williamson who owned a diamond mine in Tanzania. He was a recluse who loved dogs and the British Royal Family. His income was over £2,000,000 a year.

Some pieces of jewellery are special favourites. The Queen loves the necklace of oblong sapphires, set in diamonds, which was her wedding present from her father. She loves another wedding present too: the diamond bracelet given to her by Prince Philip. Yet more diamonds made

For grand occasions Prince Philip usually wears the splendid uniform of an Admiral of the Fleet. The large number of his medals and orders adds considerably to the magnificence. Some of his medals – as, for example, the Burma Star with Pacific Rosette – were earned during his wartime service. Others, like the Grand Cross of the British Empire, came later.

Here are some of the decorations that the Prince might be expected to wear. Atlantic Star, Star of Africa, Star of Italy, the Greek War Cross, 1939 to 1945 Star with Oak Leaf, Croix de Guerre, George VI's Coronation Medal, Elizabeth II's Jubilee Medal, the Most Noble Order of the Garter, the Most Ancient Order of the Thistle, and the Order of Merit.

Queen Elizabeth wearing the Royal Family Orders of George V and VI. The badges of these Orders are worn on the left shoulder suspended from bows of the ribands to which they are fitted. Behind the bows, platinum brooch pins are attached to the diamond Imperial Crowns which surmount the Orders. The Queen's badges are all made by Garrards. The pictures they contain are painted on ivory by Hay-Wrightson. The George V Family Order was instituted in 1911 and the George VI Family Order in 1937. There is also an Elizabeth II Family Order.

The Jubilee Necklace
Made for Queen Victoria in 1887

Queen Mary's Tiara
Bequeathed to Elizabeth II

The Williamson Pink
A wedding present from Dr Williamson

up her engagement ring, and this she always wears.

As well as jewellery, the Queen wears "Family Orders". These are exquisite miniatures of British kings, hand painted on ivory and framed in diamonds. They are pinned like brooches on the Queen's left shoulder. Her favourite miniatures are those of her father and grandfather, George V and George VI.

So her choice of ornaments is indeed dazzling. They include 10 tiaras, 19 necklaces, 17 pairs of earrings, 13 bracelets and 24 brooches — all made with some of the costliest gems in the world. But the most beautiful pieces are very much in use. On gala occasions, people expect the Queen to look truly royal, and jewels are an important part of the royal look. It cannot be easy for one figure to carry a tiara, a necklace, two brooches, earrings, two "Family Orders", a watch and two rings all at the same time. But the Queen does it — and looks magnificent.

About Royal Clothes

Ian Thomas, the dress designer, remembers an occasion when Prince Charles — aged about seven — came with his mother when she was choosing fabrics. The prince took a great liking to a silk covered with designs of little red fishes. The Queen agreed to have a dress made of it.

Norman Hartnell thought the Queen became more adventurous about her clothes as she grew older. In 1957 he designed a dazzling dress of silver lace over silver tissue for a State visit to France. "I was thrilled when she chose it," he said. And the Parisians, who had expected a more conventional outfit, were enchanted.

Comfortable shoes are a "must" for the Queen. Some she wears so often, one Australian asked: "Has the Queen only one pair?"

Writing to the Queen

My mum says I must be the only little girl in England who has the Queen for a pen pal.

Joyce, 8. English

Every week an average of over 1,000 letters, addressed to the Queen herself, arrive. The number rises when there is a special event like a royal wedding, a royal birth or a Silver Jubilee. But even in an ordinary year, the Palace receives a total of about 100,000 letters.

These letters come from all over the world. Some are on official business, the biggest number comes from people who simply want to write to the Queen. Many of the people who write to the Queen are children. They write to her about all sorts of things. Sometimes it is to get information — like the names of the royal dogs and horses. Sometimes it is just to wish her a happy birthday, or to tell her they saw her on television the night before, or to congratulate her on the birth of a grandchild.

Older people may write about a problem: perhaps a very serious problem. A new road may be planned which goes through their home; low flying aeroplanes may be making their lives a misery or, perhaps, they are unjustly accused of stealing. Although people know that the Queen no longer rules the country, the feeling remains that — in some almost magical way — she can still help.

The Queen is certainly concerned by some of these appeals. In the days when people could still be hanged, it was very hard for her to receive letters and telegrams from parents, begging her not to sign the death warrant of their son or daughter. (A little Irish girl was quite right when she wrote that "the Queen never liked to sign papers saying persons should be hong even when they very bad persons".) But, as we have said before, the Queen cannot interfere with the law. Even in the days of her great grandmother, Victoria, the only person who could reprieve a murderer was the Home Secretary.

The Queen and her staff can, however, write to a government department to see if they can help. She can forward the letter about a new road to the Department of Transport, or the letter about noisy military aircraft to the Ministry of Defence and ask for their comments. Coming from the Queen, the request gets special attention. Sometimes the answer *does* help. But she cannot interfere in any other way.

How Many Letters Does the Queen Read?

The answer is, a great many. All the letters are taken to her, unopened, in a large basket; and although there are some days when she is too busy to spend much time going through them, she likes to see as many letters as she possibly can.

The Private Secretary is in overall charge; and he and his staff make sure that the Queen sees all important official letters. Letters from children are read and answered by the Ladies in Waiting; and they will show the Queen anything that is especially nice or interesting. These letters make quite a change from the more formal correspondence and she enjoys them, but obviously it would be impossible for her to answer them all herself.

No photographs, no autographs

Probably the most usual letter sent to the Queen is a request for her photograph or autograph. But the answer has to be "no". Many photographs of the Royal Family appear in the press, and it does not seem reasonable for the Palace to send out a whole lot more. The Queen could find herself signing autographs all day and all night. Unlike nearly every other Head of State, she always signs with her own hand and never uses a stamp.

How do you address the Queen?

Many of the letters that come are simply addressed to "The Queen" or to "Queen Elizabeth". They may begin "Dear Queen", "Dear Your Majesty", or "Royal Highness". Sometimes the address is less formal. President Eduardo Frei Montalva of Chile wrote to the Queen in 1968, inviting her to come and stay. His letter began: "Good and big friend". The Queen accepted his invitation to visit Chile on a thick gold-rimmed card. Her reply was more sedate and began: "Mr President". She signed herself: "Your good friend, Elizabeth R."

The perfectly correct way to address the envelope to the Queen is:

Her Majesty The Queen
Buckingham Palace
London
SW1

The perfectly correct way to start the letter is: "Your Majesty"; and to end: "I have the honour to be Your Majesty's humble and obedient subject and servant". When her staff send memos or notes to the Queen, they write: "With my humble duty".

What answer you can expect

A few rather crazy letters get sent to the Queen. Someone may write to say he is planning to blow up Buckingham Palace or steal the state coach. Or he might suggest that the Queen should divorce Prince Philip and marry someone else. These letters are not answered; but the others will receive a reply.

Unless you are a member of the Royal Family, a personal friend, a Head of State or some other VIP, the answer will not come directly from the Queen. Remember, the Queen always signs with her own hand, so it really is not possible for her to write back to many people as each letter has to be signed by her.

The replies usually come from the Private Secretary or his assistants or the Ladies in Waiting. It will come on the official Buckingham Palace writing paper, and there will be no postage stamp on the envelope: only a number I, to indicate first class postage, and the stamp of a crown in the corner with the letters ER. The royal coat of arms will appear on the seal. The answer will usually begin: "I am commanded by the Queen to write", and it will be signed by a member of the royal household.

Dealing with all this correspondence is, as you can see, an enormous job. We have talked about some of the letters that come in; but there are, of course, thousands and thousands more. There are the requests for a royal visit, or requests for a member of the Royal Family to become patron or patronness of some charity. There are requests for all kinds of information. What exactly is the Queen's position in the Commonwealth? How did swans come to be a royal animal? Is it really true that the Princes in the Tower were murdered, not by their uncle, Richard III, but by Henry VII?

But in spite of this great mailbag, you will have seen, too, that there is always a chance the Queen will see the letter *you* write. She feels the letters are important because they help her to keep in touch with people outside the Palace. It is certainly true that many of them give her pleasure, and this is specially true of the letters from children.

Letters to the Queen

Dear Queen,

We are doing a project on you at school because we like royalty, we think you help to stop revolutions and so on. If you have time will you please send me the names of your dogs.

Yours truly,
Richard.

P.S. We have two dogs but they are not corgis.

Dear Queen Elizabeth,

Will you let me ride one of your horses? I like riding very much but my daddy says we can't afford a pony or the grass either so I thought you might share one of your many steeds with me.

Respectfully,
Gillian

The Royal Queen of England,

Please will you write and tell me the colour of your eyes. I asked my teacher and she said she hadn't the faintest idea.

Thanking you,
Mary

Dear Royal Queen,

Please will you tell me what you have for breakfast. My mum has Special K because of slimming.

Your obedient friend,
Maria

Dear Queen Elizabeth,

I saw you driving past this morning but I don't expect you saw me. I was wearing a brown cap and I did wave a lot.

Tony

To dear Queen Elizabeth,

Will you come to my birthday party next week? My mummy says you might be too busy with Prime Ministers and other things like that, but I'll send you some cake anyway.

From Eddie

Meet the Family

Top row: Prince Charles, the Queen's eldest son and heir to the throne (far left).
Prince Andrew, the Queen's third child and second in line to the throne (left).

Bottom row: Princess Anne with her husband, Captain Mark Phillips and son Peter (far left).
Prince Edward, the youngest of the Queen's four children.

Elizabeth, The Queen Mother

Born August 4th, 1900, she was the ninth child of the Earl and Countess of Strathmore and Kinghorne. She married the Duke of York on April 26th, 1923. He became King in December, 1936 and died in February, 1952.

In her eightieth year, the Queen Mother was made Lord Warden of the Cinque Ports. One of her responsibilities, she learnt, was to dispose of any whales stranded on the south-east coast of England. "All the more reason," she said, "for having a whale of a time!"

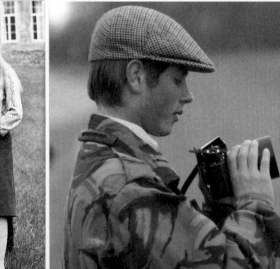

Prince Philip

Born June 10th, 1921 he was the son of Prince Andrew of Greece and Alice Battenberg. He became a naturalized British citizen in 1947 and married Princess Elizabeth in November, 1947.

Philip had an unsettled, homeless childhood. His father was charged with desertion by the Greek Government. He would almost certainly have been executed; but his cousin, King George V, stepped in. Andrew and his family were allowed to leave Greece. The baby, Philip, spent his first night at sea in an orange box — the warship could not provide a cot!

Philip went to school at Gordonstoun in Scotland. He thrived there: he was a star athlete and ended up as head boy of the school.

Princess Margaret

Born August 21st, 1930, she was the second daughter of George VI and Elizabeth. She married Antony Armstrong Jones, later Earl of Snowdon, in May 1960. They were divorced in May 1978. She has two children: David Viscount Linley, born November, 1961 and Sarah, born May, 1964.

Margaret was a naughty child. She fidgeted and giggled at solemn ceremonies. She pulled faces at the guards. She ate too many sweets. She prodded a stout visitor and asked: "Is it all you?" She mimicked important people. But she was always so lively and amusing, it was hard to scold her. The people who tried usually ended up laughing. Margaret was also very talented: a born mimic, a born dancer, able to sing any number of songs at the age of two.

Prince Charles

His Royal Highness The Prince of Wales and Earl of Chester, Duke of Cornwall and Duke of Rothesay, Earl of Carrick and Baron of Renfrew, Lord of the Isles and Great Steward of Scotland, Knight of the Garter, was born on November 14th, 1948.

As a boy Charles was gentle and rather shy. But he is now reckoned to be one of the best polo players in England and he was a good scholar at Cambridge.

He copes, gracefully, with the girls who rush from the crowds to try and kiss him. He can usually look interested and find something nice to say to all the people he has to meet on his

Queen Elizabeth the Queen Mother, in the grounds of Royal Lodge, Windsor in the year of her 80th birthday (above).

Lady Diana Spencer, the bride of Prince Charles, photographed here by Lord Snowdon. Before her engagement she worked in a school for young children.

Princess Margaret with her children, Viscount Linley and Lady Sarah Armstrong Jones (below).

public engagements.

He is known to be kind-hearted and gives his time and money generously to charity.

For years he kept the world guessing about his future Queen. But in February 1981 his engagement to the Lady Diana Spencer was announced.

Princess Anne

Born August 15th, 1950 she married Mark Phillips in November 1973. Their first child, Peter Mark Andrew, was born on November 15th, 1977.

Anne has managed to combine two careers, but it has not been easy. It's one thing to have a spare-time hobby (like George V's stamp collecting), but you don't get to win international riding events, or represent your country at the Olympics, unless you work at it very hard. To be an active member of the Royal Family is hard work too. Princess Anne has often been up at half-past five in the morning, just to get in her training on horseback as well as her public engagements.

Prince Andrew

He was born on February 17th, 1960.

Another very eligible royal bachelor — perhaps even more dreamt about by the girls than his brother, Charles. As a small boy, he was kept out of the public eye because the Queen wanted him to have as normal a childhood as possible. There was a rumour that she did it because he was mentally handicapped. It soon became clear, however, that he was very normal and *very* good looking. At school he was boisterously successful at games. He also showed a real flair for painting. As a glamorous naval officer, Andrew can have few complaints about life.

There is all the fun of being a dashing prince without the burden of being the eldest son and the heir to the throne.

Prince Edward

He was born on March 10th, 1964.

The Queen was nearly thirty-eight when the last son was born. The royal nursery, it is true, had become more easy-going; and the Queen did find it easier to spend time with the two youngest boys. It is true, too, that Edward was quieter and better behaved than Andrew. He could always get a smile out of his mother. Charles, a very kind eldest brother, spoilt him quite a lot. But the teenage prince doesn't come across as a spoilt child. Also, he is thought to be the cleverest of the four.

He has already started on his public life. He went with his parents to Canada in 1978 for the Commonwealth Games, planted a tree at Lloydminster, and descended 3,300 feet into a potash mine.

Diana, Princess of Wales

Born July 1st 1961 to the Earl and Countess Spencer. She is descended from Charles II and a distant cousin of the present Queen. It is over 300 years since an heir to the throne married an English girl. They met in a ploughed field when she was 16 and were engaged 3 years later. A "gradual" love says the Prince.

The Duke and Duchess of Gloucester at Kensington Palace shortly before their visit to Australia in 1979 (bottom right).
The Duke of Kent with his wife, Katharine and children (from left to right) George, Nicholas and Helen (top right).

Princess Alexandra

Daughter of the Duke and Duchess of Kent she was born on December 25th, 1936. She married the Hon. Angus Ogilvy on April 24th, 1963 and has two children. James Robert Bruce was born on February 1964 and Marina Victoria Alexandra was born in July 1966.

Her father was killed in the War and the family were left without much money. They were not brought up in royal splendour, and most of Alexandra's clothes were made by the village dressmaker. Like her mother, Princess Marina, she was to become a very popular royal — much in demand for public engagements. She always looks good-tempered.

Edward, Duke of Kent

Born October 9th, 1935. Married Katherine Worsley, June 1961. There are three children: George, Earl of St. Andrew's, born June 1962; Lady Helen Windsor, born April 1964; and Lord Nicholas Windsor, born July 1970.

"It is beyond question," said the Duke, "that junior members of the Royal Family ... are going to have to earn their daily bread, one way or another." Quietly and successfully, this is what he has done. He rose to be Lieutenant-Colonel in the army. Later he became Vice Chairman of the British Overseas Trade Bureau. He is reckoned to be a very hard worker for Britain — as well as for his own "daily bread".

The Duchess was the daughter of a north country squire. She had no preparation for life within the Royal Family; but she has been an outstanding success in performing public duties.

Prince Michael of Kent

Born July 1942, he married the Baroness Marie-Christina von Reibnitz in June 1978. A son, Frederick was born in April 1979.

His marriage is another sign that the Royal Family is moving with the times. Marriage to a Roman Catholic used to be nearly impossible. So was marriage to anyone who had been divorced. Prince Michael's wife is Catholic, and she has been married before. The prince was obliged, however, to renounce his right of succession to the throne. He was then sixteenth in line.

Richard, Duke of Gloucester

Born August 26th, 1944 he married Birgitte Eva Van Deurs in July 1972. They have three children: Alexander, Earl of Ulster, born in October 1974; Davina, born in November 1977; and Rose, born March 1980.

As second son he did not expect to inherit the title; but his elder brother, William, was killed in an air crash in 1972. Richard was educated at Eton and Cambridge and qualified as an architect. He married a Danish girl, daughter of a lawyer —. yet another example of the Royal Family marrying outside the conventional circle.

Princess Alexandra with her husband, the Hon. Angus Ogilvy and their children, James and Marina (top left).
Prince and Princess Michael of Kent. Prince Michael had to renounce his claim to the throne to marry (bottom left).

117

The Queen and the Commonwealth

We like the Queen because she's like the mother of a great big family.

Phillip, 12. Welsh

Many years ago, Stalin talked about the British Empire to Nancy Astor (the first woman to become a member of the British Parliament). "He was really puzzled," she remembered. "He asked how one tiny island had built an Empire that covered a quarter of the world. I told him that it can't have been might, we must have done something right!"

The British were no angels. Like most conquerors, they had wanted to make themselves richer and more powerful. But perhaps even in the early days, they had done "something right". It had long been understood that a good monarch ruled with the goodwill of the people. The same principle held when the people lived in faraway countries and it was the British Government — not the Monarch — who ruled.

Britain tried, in general, to make things better for the countries of the Empire. They had helped them to develop new industries, modern methods of farming and better medical care. They had also insisted on the British system of justice. Anyone accused of a crime was entitled to a fair trial and it was the same trial for rich or poor.

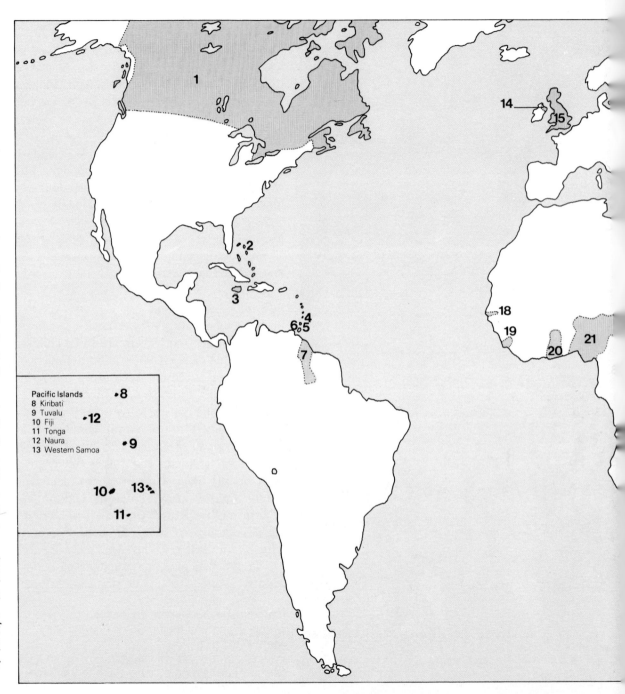

Pacific Islands
8 Kiribati
9 Tuvalu
10 Fiji
11 Tonga
12 Naura
13 Western Samoa

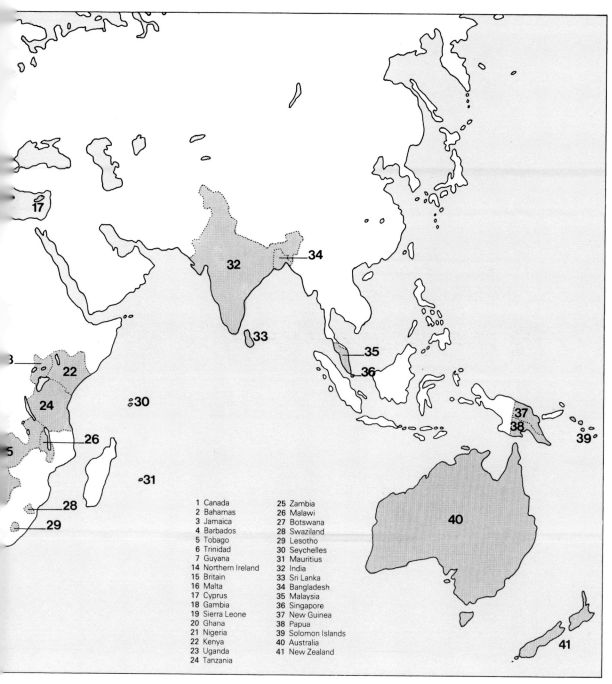

1	Canada	25	Zambia
2	Bahamas	26	Malawi
3	Jamaica	27	Botswana
4	Barbados	28	Swaziland
5	Tobago	29	Lesotho
6	Trinidad	30	Seychelles
7	Guyana	31	Mauritius
14	Northern Ireland	32	India
15	Britain	33	Sri Lanka
16	Malta	34	Bangladesh
17	Cyprus	35	Malaysia
18	Gambia	36	Singapore
19	Sierra Leone	37	New Guinea
20	Ghana	38	Papua
21	Nigeria	39	Solomon Islands
22	Kenya	40	Australia
23	Uganda	41	New Zealand
24	Tanzania		

Sometimes the British behaved badly. George III's government tried to force unfair taxes on the Americans. The result was a disaster for him and his Government, and America was lost as a colony. Later monarchs, however, were to establish a special link between themselves and the people of the Empire.

When George V decided to have a second coronation in India, some of his Ministers wondered if this would be popular with the Indian people. The answer was "yes". The Indians turned out in their millions to greet their King and Queen. It was one of the great successes in his reign.

The link between the Empire and the Crown remained. It became clear that the countries in the Empire wanted their independence, wanted the freedom to govern themselves. It also became clear that Britain was far less wealthy and powerful than in Victorian days. The country was therefore less able to give practical help and other benefits to the Commonwealth.

If Britain had been a republic, with a changing President, it is likely that the Empire would have vanished as completely as the Empire of Rome. But the feeling for the "Mother Country" persisted. The "Mother" who had once been symbolized by Victoria, was still symbolized by the Royal Family, by her great-granddaughter, Elizabeth II. The Empire became the Commonwealth largely because so many countries felt able to accept her as their constitutional Head.

The Commonwealth is like an enormous club. There is no longer any question of British rule. The countries have their own governments and have chosen of their own free will to become members of the club.

The Commonwealth countries are: Great Britain and Northern Ireland, Australia, New Zealand, Jamaica, the Bahamas, Barbados, Canada, Fiji, Dominica, Grenada, Mauritius, Papua New Guinea, St Lucia, Tuvalu (formerly the Ellice Islands), the Solomon Islands, Malaysia, Tonga, Lesotho, Swaziland, Bangladesh, Botswana, Cyprus, Gambia, Ghana, Malawi, Kenya, Nigeria, Nauru, Sierra Leone, the Seychelles, Sri Lanka, Tanzania, Uganda, India, Guyana, Zambia, Kiribati (formerly the Gilbert Islands), Western Samoa, Zimbabwe, St Vincent and Vanuatu (formerly the New Hebrides). As you can see, they are nations of many different races. They occupy about ten million square miles of the earth.

It is said that the Queen is one of the most travelled women in the world; and she certainly feels that visits to the Commonwealth countries are a very important part of her job. Family reasons are not allowed to interfere. In 1959 she was expecting her third child, Andrew; but that did not stop her travelling 18,000 miles in Canada. Still earlier, in 1952, she had found it terribly hard to say goodbye to her sick father. But a big tour of Africa, Australia and New Zealand had been planned and had to go ahead.

Every year, she is anxious to fit in more visits. She has sat on the ground, eating with her fingers, at a banquet in Tonga. She has struggled with chopsticks in Singapore and with raw fish in Fiji. During Silver Jubilee Year she travelled 56,000 miles to visit 13 countries.

The Queen once said the Commonwealth was "like an iceberg, except that it's not cold". She believes the official meetings between the Government heads and the Commonwealth Conference are only the tip of the iceberg. All the time, warm, friendly, unofficial contacts are going on beneath the surface. It is indeed that friendship which keeps the whole thing afloat.

Queen Elizabeth II with the Heads of Government and leading representatives from thirty-two Commonwealth countries pose for this picture in the Music Room of Buckingham Palace before attending a banquet in the magnificent Throne Room of the Palace. The Queen's guests pictured with her are (left to right): Front row, Dr Hastings Banda (Malawi); Shri Moraji Desai (India); Mr Malcolm Fraser (Australia); Mr Michael Manley (Jamaica); Archbishop Makarios (Cyprus); Mr James Callaghan (Britain); Dr Kenneth Kaunda (Zambia); Major-General Aiaur Rahman (Bangladesh); Mr Robert Muldoon (New Zealand); Brigadier Shehu Yar' Adua (Nigeria). Second row, Mr Michael Somare (Papua New Guinea); Dr Siaka Stevens (Sierra Leone); Sir Seewoosagur Ramgoolam (Mauritius); Mr Tom Adams (Barbados); Mr Eric Gairy (Grenada); Mr Aboud Jumbe (Tanzania); General F. Akuffo (Ghana); Mr Lynden Pindling (Bahamas); Prince Tatafehi Tu' ipelehake (Tonga); Back row, Taisi Tupuola Efi (Western Samoa); Datuk Hussein Bin Onn (Malaysia); Sir Damisese Mara (Fiji); Dr Leabau Jonathan (Lesotho); Vice-President D. Arap Moi (Kenya); Mr Lee Kuan Yew (Singapore); Mr Feliz Bandaranaike.(Sri Lanka); Mr Fred Wills (Guyana); Colonel Maphevu Dlamini (Swaziland); Mr John Donaldson (Trinidad and Tobago); Sir Dawda Jawara (Gambia); Sir Seretse Khama (Botswana); Mr Pierre Trudeau (Canada).

If Stalin were alive today, he might ask a rather different question. He might be even more puzzled than he had been during the talk with Lady Astor. "How", he might ask, "has one tiny island persuaded about 900 million people to *stay* together?" Lady Astor's reply could still be the same, "It can't be might. They must have done something right." Many people feel it is the Monarchy, above all, which has done something right.

When Ministers from Commonwealth countries come to Britain, they will, of course, have meetings with members of the Government or with Civil Servants. But they will also visit Buckingham Palace and talk to the Queen; and it is said, again and again, that this is the most "special" part of their visit. They like the unchanging nature of the Monarchy; and the affection, inspired by Victoria, still remains. *Victoria stayed the same*. Some tribes in Africa even thought she was immortal; and when she died, they said a new star had appeared in the sky.

There is something special, too, about the Queen's frequent visits to the Commonwealth countries. Lady Foot, whose husband was then Governor General of Jamaica, remembers the Queen's thoughtfulness for people in the crowds. An old lady was standing by the roadside with a bunch of flowers she wanted to present. The royal car passed before the Queen could tell the driver to stop; but she turned and gestured to Lady Foot who was following behind. "We knew what the Queen meant us to do and we stopped and spoke to the old lady and took her little bunch and her name and address." One of the first things the Queen asked when she got out of the car was: "did you thank the old lady? did you ask for her address? I am so sorry I did not see her in time but we will write and thank her."

Here are some examples of the Royal Arms which can only be displayed by trades people, officially appointed to supply members of the Royal Family.

Royal Warrant holders to HM Queen Elizabeth II.

Royal Warrant holders to
HM Queen Elizabeth II
in Scotland.

Royal Warrant holders to
Elizabeth the Queen Mother.

Royal Warrant holders to
HM the Queen Mother
in Scotland.

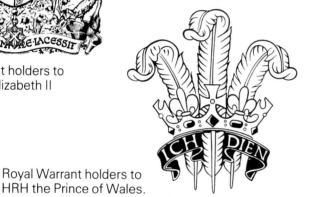

Royal Warrant holders to
HRH the Prince of Wales.

Royal Warrant holders to
HRH the Duke of Edinburgh.

Royal Warrants

For hundreds of years there have been tradesmen who supplied the monarch with various goods and services. There were Purveyors of "Beeves, Mutton and Veales"; there were also royal button-makers, sword cutters, pin-makers, mole-takers, organ-builders and whip makers.

Royal Charters were granted to guilds who supplied the Monarch. The first on record was given by Henry II in 1155 to the Weavers Company. But the present system of Royal Warrants only came in during the reign of George V. Before then, almost everyone could claim to be a royal supplier. Now the number is strictly controlled. About 850 tradesmen have the right to display the Royal Arms together with the words "By Appointment".

A local shop at Balmoral. Even small shops can hold a Royal Warrant if they supply goods to the Royal Family.

GOODBYE!

When other kings come tumbling down
And breaking all their lovely crowns

We know our Queen will still be there,
It's lucky that she has an heir.

She's ruled us for a nice long time
With Philip standing right behind,
A better husband she won't find
And what's more, he speaks his mind.

Dear Queen Elizabeth goodbye,
At the end of all these pages.

And please whatever you do
keep reigning
For ages
      And ages
            And AGES!

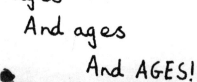

William I (1066–87)
the Conquerer

William II (1087–1100)
Killed hunting

Henry I (1100–35)
A strong king

Stephen (1135–54)
Fought Matilda
for the Crown

Matilda (Born 1102 died 1167)
First woman to claim
the English Crown

Henry II (1154–89)

Richard I (1189–99)

John (1199–1216)

Henry III (1216–72)

Edward I (1272–1307)

Edward II (1307–27)

Edward III (1327–77)

Edward, the Black Prince
(Born 1330 died 1363)

Richard II (1377–99)

Henry IV (1399–1413)
Deposed and murdered
Richard II

Henry V (1413–22)
Conquered France

Henry VI (1422–61)
and (1470–71)
Murdered

Edward IV (1461–70)
and (1471–83)
Very handsome

Edward V (Born 1471 died 1483)
Murdered in the Tower

Richard III (1483–85)
Suspected murderer of
the princes in the Tower

Henry VII (1485–1509)

Prince Arthur (Died 1502)
Eldest son of Henry VII

Henry VIII (1509–47)

Edward VI (1547–53)
Brilliant scholar

Mary I (1553–58)
"Bloody Mary"

Elizabeth I (1558–1603)
A great queen

Catherine of Aragon
Henry VIII's 1st wife

Anne Boleyn
Henry VIII's 2nd wife
Beheaded

Jane Seymour
Henry VIII's 3rd wife

Anne of Cleves
Henry VIII's 4th wife
Divorced

Catherine Howard
Henry VIII's 5th wife
Beheaded

Catherine Parr
Henry VIII's 6th wife
Survived Henry

ALL ABOUT THE ROYAL FAMILY

James I (1603–25)

Prince Henry (Died 1612)
James' eldest son

Charles I (1625–49)
Beheaded

Charles II (1660–85)

James II (1685–88)
Deposed

William III and Mary II (1688–94)
William reigned alone until 1702

Anne (1702–14)

George I (1714–27)
Spoke no English

George II (1727–60)
A harsh father

George III (1760–1820)
"Farmer George"

George IV (1820–30)
A great builder

William IV (1830–37)
Bluff sailor

Victoria (1837–1901)
Only Monarch to celebrate
a Diamond Jubilee

Edward VII (1901–10)

George V (1910–36)
Great stamp collector

Edward VIII (1936)
Abdicated
Died in 1972

George VI (1936–1952)
Married Elizabeth Bowes-Lyon

Elizabeth II (the present Queen)
with her husband, Philip

Index